CHEIROS WORLD PREDICTIONS

CHEIROS WORLD PREDICTIONS

CHEIRO

GYAN

Published by

Gyan Publishing House
5, Ansari Road
Daryaganj, New Delhi-110002
Phone: 011-47034999, 9811692060
E-mail: books@gyanbooks.com

Distribution Network
gyanbooks.com
India, USA, Canada, UK, Australia

ISBN: 978-93-7316-654-4 (PB)

First Published, 1931

2nd Impression 2025

Printed at: Gyan Press, Delhi.

CHEIROS WORLD PREDICTIONS
Arthur: CHEIRO

CHEIRO'S WORLD PREDICTIONS

NEW AND ENLARGED EDITION

CHEIRO'S WORLD PREDICTIONS

THE FATE OF EUROPE
THE FUTURE OF THE U.S.A.
THE COMING WAR OF NATIONS
THE RESTORATION OF THE JEWS

CANADA, U.S.A., ARGENTINA, BRAZIL, CHILE, COLUMBIA, ECUADOR, PERU, VENEZUELA, ETC.
ENGLAND, IRELAND, GERMANY, FRANCE, ITALY, SPAIN, RUSSIA, CHINA, JAPAN, ETC.
SOUTH AFRICA, MEXICO, AUSTRALIA, NEW ZEALAND, AFGHANISTAN, BURMAH, TURKEY, PALESTINE, INDIA, ETC.
NORWAY, SWEDEN, DENMARK, ROUMANIA, POLAND, EASTERN EUROPE EGYPT, ETC.

HERBERT JENKINS LIMITED
3 YORK STREET, ST. JAMES'S
LONDON S.W.1

AUTHOR'S PREFACE
TO
NEW AND ENLARGED EDITION

It has been my privilege to visit the United States and other parts of the North American Continent many times since I first visited there in 1893.

This is not the place for me to write about the almost incredible advancement and prosperity that has occurred in these countries during the past forty years. I only allude to the length of time in answer to critics in the Press who have considered my Predictions in Chapters VI and VII, relating to the still greater future of the North American Continent, as too optimistic to be verified.

My revised opinion is that I have not been optimistic enough and that in my calculations as to the "New Age" in which the world entered about A.D. 1766, at the same time when the United States obtained her Independence and became a Nation, is indicated a date in the history of civilisation of such importance, and in such keeping with those God-designed cycles of Time explained by me in Chapter XII, that no prophetic vision could be equal to the task of picturing the power and wealth of the North American Continent in another span of the next few hundred years.

In Chapter V I have set out my reasons for stating that ages before North America was discovered, this part of the world was placed in what is called the "First House of Air" in the Zodiacal plan of control of the countries of the Earth.

In the part of this book dealing with the future of the United States, I have given this as one of the reasons why this country, more than all others, must dominate in "the conquest of the Air", but in revising these proofs for this new and enlarged Edition, I consider I did not lay enough emphasis on the fact that in no other part of the world has Helium been discovered in such quantities as in the oil wells of the United States. This non-inflammable gas which has such decided advantages over hydrogen or coal gas for airships, is even at this date being extracted daily by many thousands of cubic feet from certain oil wells in the States, and stored in steel cylinders for such purposes by the U.S. Government.

When the time comes, as it undoubtedly will come, and is rapidly coming, the United States will be in a position to exploit the "Kingdom of the Air" not only by Aeroplanes, but by Airships with privileges that no other Nation in the world possesses.

I have also been called to task by some sections of the Press on the length of space I have devoted in this book to the future of the Jews, and my predictions as so the influence and rôle they will play in the coming problems of civilisation.

Some papers have gone so far as to accuse me of deliberately making "a propaganda in favour of the Jews without an equal in recent history."

It is, therefore, only fair to my readers to make the statement once and for all—that I am not a Jew, nor have I, as far as I can trace, any Jewish blood in my veins.

As a Student of Occultism, which it should be remembered is the foundation of all religions, I could not allow myself to have a bias towards one race more than another, and if I have in the course of these pages laid considerable stress on the future of such a Nation as the United States, or predicted the return of the Jews to power, I have done so from a genuine and conscientious belief that such are the indications and trend of conditions, and as they appeared to me, so was it my duty without caring for fear or favour, to make them known to the public in the pages of these "World Predictions."

"CHEIRO."

PREFACE

IT is only fair to state that I first received the Manuscript of "World Predictions" from "Cheiro" in October, 1925.

As many of these Predictions were of a nature that concerned deeply the future of the British Empire and other nations, I advised their appearance in newspapers having a world-wide circulation. I found, however, that the majority of editors would not undertake their publication unless they were so cut about and restricted that the warnings they contained would be rendered useless. In nearly every case these manuscripts were returned with a note invariably saying, "too sensational for our columns" or words to that effect, and so in the end I advised their publication in book form.

In the MS. that was sent to me in October, 1925, "Cheiro" among other things, very clearly foretold the Treaty made in the following March, 1926, between Soviet Russia and Germany, the breaking out of Civil War in China and its effect on English interests. The

General Strike in Great Britain of May, 1926, together with the extraordinary number of fires that destroyed large private mansions all over England during that year. He also foretold the commencement of series of Earthquakes in countries that for hundreds of years have been more or less free from such occurrences, and nine months in advance indicated clearly the one that occurred in the Channel Islands in July, 1926, and that it "would be followed by another over a large area of England in the Autumn of the same year."

During the time that I have had the MS. of the following book under consideration, I have examined the numerous instances that are on record of previous predictions made by this "Modern Seer" and I can say that their remarkable accuracy is almost beyond belief. In a Preface of this kind I have only space at my disposal to call attention to a few which are of general interest, and which were made a considerable time before the events took place; such as the Boer War, the death of Queen Victoria, the Entente Cordiale between France and England, at time a when such an event was the last thing that could be expected. The assassination of King Humbert of Italy, the attempt on the life of the Shah of Persia in Paris in 1900, the exact year, month and day, of the death of King Edward VII, the date of the Great War "in the midsummer of 1914," that "its duration would be about four years" and its end "the collapse of the Central Powers of Europe and the break-up of Russia as an Empire."

Another of "Cheiro's" remarkable predictions made several years before its fulfilment was "the downfall of the Czar and his massacre, together with every member of his immediate family."

Other accurate foreshadowings of the future are now matters of history, such as his warning to W. T. Stead, editor of the *Review of Reviews*, made nine months in advance, of his death by drowning in April, 1912. His intimation fully four years in advance to Lord Russell of Killowen of the date when he would wear the robes of Lord Chief Justice of England for the first time, and that most astonishing prediction to Lord Kitchener when, as Colonel Kitchener and a comparatively unknown soldier, he was told by "Cheiro," first in 1887 and again in 1894 (when Kitchener gave him a signed impression of his hand), that he would have the heavy responsibility of the War of 1914 on his shoulders and would meet his death not on the battlefield as a soldier might have expected, but *by disaster at Sea in his sixty-sixth year*.

The above examples are but a few that I select out of general interest, many thousands of others are verified by letters from people in all ranks of life who have consulted "Cheiro" during his professional career—now closed to the general public.

At different times in the history of the world there are records of "Seers" and "prophets" whose predictions have been remarkably fulfilled, but nearly all of these are isolated instances. There is, in fact, no record in history, past or present, of any other man who for twenty-one years made the unique reputation that this man made, and not in one country alone, but all over the world. But the day came at last when his own prediction of his retirement had to be fulfilled. Nerves of steel could not stand for ever the continual responsibility of advising other lives from morning to night. Yet it was, I feel sure, with many a pang of regret that "Cheiro" gave up the personal contact with his individual consultants, and sought the still wider field of influence that is now given to him by the power of the pen.

Versed in the knowledge of occult studies as few men have ever been, with long years of experience of the desires, hopes and fears of humanity behind him, he is in the position to-day of a teacher who has not only the great lesson of life to teach, gathered from those thousands of lives who came so intimately into contact with his own, but as well he has a message to the world at large, as is shown by the foreshadowing of the destiny of nations which he sets out in clear unmistakable language in the pages of this book, now presented to the public for the first time.

Before going to press the Author has taken the opportunity of making an interesting addition to Chapter VII, regarding the exploitation of rubber plantations by American capital which he predicted would occur when he sent the MS. of this book for publication in 1925. He has also made a valuable addition to his "Predictions" in Part III, by forecasting "Coming Earthquakes, Subsidences and Upheavals" which, even while we are going to Press, are being borne out to a remarkable

In this revised and enlarged edition the Author has added an entire new Part II, of predictions concerning the immediate future of the principal nations of the World.

THE EDITOR.

CONTENTS

PART I

CHAPTER I

THE FATE OF NATIONS

CHAPTER II

THE FATE OF NATIONS (*continued*)

CHAPTER III

THE HOUSE OF WINDSOR AND ITS DESTINY

CHAPTER IV

THE BRITISH EMPIRE IN ITS WORLD ASPECT

Chapter V

Chapter VI

Chapter VII

Chapter VIII

PART I

PART I

THE ORIGIN OF GREAT BRITAIN
THE INFLUENCE OF THE JEWS
IN
BRITISH HISTORY
THE UNITED STATES OF AMERICA
AND
THE FUTURE OF THE
PRINCIPAL NATIONS OF THE WORLD

Chapter I

THE FATE OF NATIONS

IS IT PEACE OR WAR FOR GREAT BRITAIN, EUROPE, AND THE WORLD IN GENERAL?

I WILL endeavour to explain as clearly as the written word will allow, how it may be possible under certain conditions to foresee coming events in connection with the destiny of nations.

Such a statement will undoubtedly arouse criticism in many quarters. In view of this, I simply ask those who may read this book, to lay aside for the moment prejudice against the idea that the future can be foreseen, and whatever bias they may have from the standpoint of religion.

If they will do this they will find that my writings are not anti-religious, but, on the contrary, of such a nature that "their God is also my God," and that what I teach can only in the end increase that reverence for the Divine Essence that is the central and controlling thought in all religions, no matter in what name or in what form they may worship God.

That there is design, *and intelligent design, underlying, developing and controlling* all things, has been admitted by every scientist, philosopher or thinker who has ever given a thought to the subject.

The working out of design in any form is a slow process. On a loom the threads have to be prepared and placed in position, the commencement is nebulous and vague.

In the brain of the weaver alone *the thought-picture* is clear and decided. In this mind the design not only *exists* but it stands out in all its perfection. The warp and weft, the flying shuttle, the colours he is about to use, are to him only the means to an ultimate end.

As Time goes on fragments of the thought-picture begin to become apparent, and, finally, *to some eyes who may be privileged to see it*, the design itself is grasped *long before it has any form or meaning to others.*

I give this as an illustration of the line of thought I am going to pursue. In making predictions for the various countries of the world, the method I employ is the following:

Apart from the study of what is called Mundane Astrology, I employ a system of mental concentration which I learned during my sojourn in India and followed up in later years in my studies in Occultism. In using this method I endeavour to absorb the past history of whatever country is occupying my attention, paying special attention to the periodical cycles that appear to influence its destiny.

Combining this with my knowledge of Astrology and the influence of the changing Signs of the Zodiac and their planetary relationship, I arrive at conclusions that might never arrest the attention of those who follow ordinary methods of observation and deduction.

That my method is a successful one has been amply proven by the many predictions I have made which have been verified in after years.

In order to save space, I will presume that my readers are aware that the Study of the Heavens, otherwise Astrology, is as old as Religion itself. Records go to prove that as far back as Seth, the third son of Adam, the constellations were already known and the influence of the twelve divisions of the Zodiac on humanity had already been observed. If proof is wanted for this statement we can find it in the third chapter of the first book of Josephus, where the famous Hebrew historian writes "Man lived so long before the Flood that he learned the arts and sciences especially Astrology and Geometry," and later he states that Abraham, when he sojourned in Egypt, "taught the Egyptians the knowledge of *Astrology*." Also from Josephus we learn that

Seth, foreseeing the Flood, engraved the principles of his astrological knowledge on two pillars of stone for the benefit of after ages, and the great historian goes on to relate that in his own time he saw "one of the pillars still standing in Syria."

I am only mentioning these things *en passant* for the benefit of those who may not have the time to study such subjects, and to show that the ideas handed down to us by Astrology are as old as is the world itself.

As this book is not written as a defence of this ancient science I will not take up the time of my readers in tracing its history through the ages, however interesting and instructive that might be, but I will proceed at once to a practical application of its rules in connection with the destiny of the principal nations of the world.

The origin of the meaning given to the twelve divisions of the Zodiac and the qualities of the nine planets that appear to have such an important influence on humanity, is completely lost in antiquity, the fact alone remaining that the rules laid down bear the same relation to our modern existence as they did in the most far off æons of time.[1]

[1]The great English Astronomer Newton, writing about the origin of Astrology, says "The Egyptians determined the length of the solar year and fixed the solstices in the reigns of Ammon and Memnon, and the King of Sais, by the assistance of a priest of Egypt, created the science of Astrology, grounding it on the aspects of the Planets."

How and when the ancient Masters of this study formulated these rules it is impossible to estimate. One theory is that in those ages when we are told "God talked with man," He revealed the Divine plan of the universe to certain men or sects who were ready to receive this knowledge.[1]

The part that concerns us is, that as these great students of nature handed down to posterity the exact calculation as to the "Precession of the Equinoxes" being a period of 25,850 years,[2] they may be equally correct in their other statements as to the influence of

[1]According to Oriental records the birth of Astrology is coexistent with the creation of the world. They state that Nacrawonsch, the son of Misraim, excelled in Astrology and commenced the first dynasty of his race who were all skilled in the mystic arts. The most celebrated of the Misraimiam Princes was Naerasch, who represented in figures and images the twelve signs of the Zodiac.

Pharaoh, the last Prince of this dynasty, endeavoured to destroy Noah, believing that by so doing he would prevent the deluge, but he was himself with his whole family swept away by the Flood.

Efilimoun alone, the chief Astrologer of the day, foreseeing the desolation that was coming, acknowledged the truth of the warning preached by Noah, and was admitted into the Ark with all his family. Forming an alliance with Noah and his descendants he became the ancestor of twenty-six kings of the second dynasty of Egypt and built the city of Memphis. Misraim, his son, was the depositary of all the magical and astrological secrets of the first ages of the world.

[2]Herschel makes this calculation 25,870 years. Chambers, another great authority, works out 25,817 as the period of the Precession of the Equinoxes. I have taken 25,850 years as the mean between these two calculations. Seventy years and nine months is as nearly as can be estimated a *day* of the great equinox year, which it will be noted is in exact accordance with the verse in Psalms xc, 10, "The days of our years are three score years and ten (70), and if by reason of strength they be fourscore years, yet is their strength labour and sorrow." The

the planets on the destiny of peoples and nations.

Without further preamble, I will now endeavour to show what this strange study of the heavens foreshadows for the principal nations of the earth.

What of the future?

This is the question which again and again rushes into the minds of individuals, and, as individuals are but units of great nations, so the same fateful interrogation is vaguely indulged in when the coming years are anticipated, especially now that war is still a memory, and the civilised world yet labours in the trough of difficult post-war times.

Great statesmen and those who must guide the helm of nations question the future with anxious hearts. The storm is past, but the waves run high. Are there rocks and shoals concealed beneath the heaving waters, that may once more bring disaster to Humanity—disaster that must of necessity be more scientifically terrible than even the past years of Carnage?

---

nine months over the 70 years is the precise period from conception to birth.

The exact rate of the "Precession of the Equinoxes" has therefore been so wonderfully determined by the "Great Geometrician of the Universe" that it indicates the length of human life—which "is but a day" and is another example of how man is influenced by the Divine order of the Celestial bodies, which thought is so beautifully expressed in that prayer we are taught from our earliest infancy, "Thy Will be done on earth as it is in Heaven."

In the old days, monarchs and despots applied to their astrologers and soothsayers to scan the heavens and read in the glowing planets the destinies of nations. From Zannes and Zambres, who stood before Egypt's Pharaoh and read the decrees of Fate, to the famous Dr. John Dee who laid before Queen Elizabeth a scroll of events that were minutely fulfilled in following years, multitudes of "Seers" have predicted national events, risings and fallings, and the ebb and flow of dynasties.

In these days of scientific knowledge people may smile to think that the Future of Nations can still be foreseen by a study of planetary influences. But I will boldly say, after long years of investigation, *that such a thing is possible.* The heavenly bodies rule the Fates of Individuals; the same planets guide and govern *the destinies of Nations.*

First, I will explain as simply as possible why I predict events, startling perhaps and full of interest, immediately concerning Great Britain, the United States and other nations. Then I shall show the reason why, in my judgment, certain national movements and groupings together of races must be seen taking place among other countries. And in the consideration will be found emerging the profoundly interesting speculation that must grip every reader: *Is it war or peace for the world?*

That the two great English speaking countries of the world are instruments carrying out the purpose of Destiny, there can be no question. But will they be drawn together in the immediate future to stand shoulder to shoulder for those standard qualities of Humanity that are the rock foundations of civilisation? That is the question which concerns all.

I suppose it is not generally realised that nations, as well as individuals, since long past ages, have their own Zodiacal sign. And it is highly significant, *how significant* we cannot yet fully realise, that the sign governing London as the capital of the British Empire, literally the heart of the Empire, is what is known as the Sign of Gemini; and it is revealingly significant that this same Sign *governs the United States*.

Let me explain another strange coincidence, strange, that is, to our superficial thought, which must have a remarkable bearing on the future.

The Sign of Gemini is also known as the First House of the planet Mercury. This planet, since the most distant ages, has been known to all students of occultism as the signification of everything that represents mental activity and especially commerce, business, science, calculation and enterprise.

London has been the centre of commerce, business, banking and enterprise for hundreds of years. In more recent times the United States has steadily followed the lead of London, *not in one city alone*, but in all her cities and towns from the Atlantic to the Pacific—*for the whole of North America is under the Sign of Gemini.*

Therefore, in spite of the wide varieties of climate, the fusion of different races, the deviation in national character, etc., there is *one bond* in common that will hold England and America together, in spite of petty and perhaps irritating differences that may arise from time to time between the nations. That bond is the greatest and most potent that can be found—namely, that of their Zodiacal affinity.

These two great nations are *compelled, by a magnetic occult force*, to join together not only to protect their nationality and their interests, but all they as nations stand for in the great plan of Progress and Humanity.

Because London—England's heart—is governed by Gemini (the same sign that rules the United States), during the War of Independence the feeling in London and in the Parliament at Westminster was in favour of Peace. Pitt's great speech in the Commons against the continuation of this "fratricidal and senseless war of blood and butchery" was acclaimed at Westminster as ringing true, except among the Court Party, the head of which was George the Third, who was clearly indicated by Astrology as an instrument to bring about the independence of the United States.

We will now turn for a moment to another side of these observations and consider the Zodiacal affinity of England with European nations. The remainder of England, that is England with the exception of London, the heart, is influenced by the Zodiacal Sign of Aries—the First House of the planet Mars. And, looking out among the neighbouring nations we find that exactly *the same house and warlike planet* govern Germany.

Therefore, in spite of all that has happened in the past, it is evident that England and Germany are intended by Nature *to be allies instead of enemies*.

Even a superficial survey will attest the naturalness of this, when considered from an impartial, non-political point of view.

England and Germany have the same dogged obstinacy of purpose, solidity, hard-headed business qualities, and keen pursuit of science. They are the only two nationalities in Europe that have *blended together in past history*. The Saxons or Norsemen were the forebears of what is known as the Anglo-Saxon race and history records that they made no less than six settlements in England from A.D. 449 to about A.D. 547. They drove the native Britons out of the country to the extreme Western part which they called

Wales, the name Welsh being even to-day *a Saxon term for foreigners.*

The Normans who came later were not French as is commonly supposed, but were the descendants of Norsemen from Denmark and Northern Germany, who, after laying waste the Northern part of France, forced the King of France to marry his daughter to Rollo the Sea King, and give the name of Normandy (derived from Norsemen or Northmen) to the part they had conquered.

This is not an idle repetition of History, but it has a significance that can hardly be over-estimated.

In later years History repeated itself, and German princes occupied the British throne when George the First came as the first of the Hanoverian Kings. In so doing he united the Houses of Hanover and Guelph, until King George the Fifth, under the stress of conditions caused by the Great War, on the 17th July, 1917, by Royal Proclamation, declared himself no longer Hanover or Guelph, but of the House of Windsor.

Such a mingling of nations has never occurred before, and, for Occult reasons, as I will explain, could not occur between France and England, or England and Italy; it could not occur in Elizabeth's day between England and Spain, and the short period when Philip of Spain was Consort of Queen Mary was fraught with utter misery for the English nation. How significant were the words of Dr. John Dee, the Astrologer, when he first heard of the alliance between the English Lion and the Asturian Leopard—"Woe to the two Nations! Sorrow and dolour! Disaster by Water and persecution by Fire. And our Queen shall die childless." The persecution of the Protestants by Queen Mary, her unhappy disappointment with regard to the cradle, and later the wreck of Spain's maritime hopes in the loss of the "Invincible Armada" fulfilled the great Astrologer's words and was the death blow to any hope of uniting England and Spain.

To-day statesmen are keenly watching the trend of events governing the relations between France and England. Comrades in the Great War—or I should prefer to say Allies forced into a common line of action—to-day there is irritation, bitterness, and a sense of growing isolation between the two nations. Money talks loudly, and War Debts fret the soul of France, while England remains outwardly stolid but actually chafed by a position that proves there is no real union between Paris and London. The reason for this is the following:—

Paris—the heart of France—is governed by the planet Mercury in its *Second House, which is the Sign of Virgo*. This in itself has a remarkable significance that cannot be overlooked in considering past, present and future events as affecting the Great Powers.

In studying these matters, it must be borne in mind that countries as a whole have often a sign of the Zodiac governing them which may be distinct and different from the sign or planet that governs their capital. This is peculiarly so in the case of both England and France.

England as a country, is governed by the Sign of Aries, which is called the "House of Mars (positive)" and her symbol is astrologically that of the Ram, while her capital, London, is governed by the Sign of Gemini, with the planet Mercury (positive) in its First House.

France as a country is governed by the Sign of Leo, and her symbol astrologically is the Lion, while her capital, Paris, is governed by the Sign of Virgo *with the planet Mercury in its Second House as its ruler.* This is a "feminine" indication with all the changeability and impulsive qualities usually associated with the nature of a woman.

If this is carefully considered it will explain a great deal. In symbolism the Lion and the Ram are antagonistic to one another. Let it be remembered that England only put the Lion on her Standard after she was overrun by the Normans, the Lion being on the

Norman Standard as it had been since the days of Rollo the Sea King, the first Duke of Normandy, and is to the present day.

As I explained earlier, the United States is also ruled by the Sign of Gemini with Mercury (positive), the same as London, consequently this combination will be continually involved with intrigues with Paris over finance, commerce and business matters, and because as Paris has the weaker sign of Mercury in its Second House she will become more and more influenced by London and the United States in all matters of finance.

Outside of Paris, speaking from a Zodiacal standpoint, France *as a country* will be antagonistic to England *as a country*, and there can never be unity or any real friendship between them.

The Zodiacal sign of France as a country being Leo, gives the symbolism of the noble attributes of the Lion to her people, such as courage, chivalry, dashing valour, strong individuality, but an "aloneness" of character which will prevent her having Allies for any length of time, while Paris, her capital, under Mercury (negative) in Virgo will have the weaker Mercurial qualities denoted by this combination, such as versatility of plans, love of change, unsettled moods, perpetual tendencies towards change of Government and lack of stability in finance, and in purpose.

It will thus be seen that England cannot mate with France, their planetary vibrations not being in harmony, consequently trouble and vexation must ensue. A backward glance at the working out of the much heralded *Entente Cordiale* reveals its own story. Such an Entente cannot last, as coming years will show in a most decided fashion.

Let us now turn to Belgium, the cause, be it remembered, of Great Britain at the commencement of the Great War drawing the sword on the side of France. The British Cabinet was not decided in favour of intervention up to the very last moment, and the French Ambassador, Monsieur Cambon, hung upon the steps of Downing Street in an agony of apprehension concerning the apparent vacillation of the British Government, while German troops were marching through Luxemburg in the early fateful days of August, 1914.

But Belgium is governed by the Sign of Gemini—London's own Zodiacal sign. So that, although the rest of England, being under Aries as already explained, *was decidedly averse to a war with Germany*, as is amply attested by historical retrospect, the Cabinet *in London* made the decision, issued the ultimatum to Germany, and at midnight on the

4th of August the two nations were in a state of war.[1]

In contemplating the destinies of the nations in the years now opening before us, the affinities of various groups of nations to different planets must now be closely considered.

Thus, England, Germany, Denmark, Western Poland, Palestine, Syria and Japan are governed by the Sign of Aries with Mars as ruler of that sign; it is inevitable therefore that these countries must sooner or later be drawn together and intermingle in one another's affairs. The greatest danger in these countries must come from nations ruled by Saturn, the planet equally powerful with Mars. Let us therefore see the nations that are ruled by it.

They are: Lower Austria, Czecho-Slovakia, Yugo-Slavia, Westphalia, Greece, Bulgaria, Egypt, India, the Punjab, Afghanistan, Tibet, China, and Russia—an interesting combination of diverse people.

What, it may be questioned, are the indications from an astrological viewpoint of the trend of events in the immediate future?

I am sorry to record, after a very careful series of calculations and deductions, that the outlook *is ominous in the extreme.* Moreover,

[1] In 1815, one hundred years previous to the last war, England sent her troops to Belgium to the defeat of Napoleon and the French Army at the battle of Waterloo

the unfavourable signs, that in my judgment will lead to fresh war, will commence to be manifest *by secret treaties and combinations* brought about during 1926 and continuing through the following years.

It must not be forgotten that although the Great War did not begin so far as open hostilities went, until August, 1914, it was in the Spring of 1913 that the Powers behind the Thrones of Europe had decided that "War was Inevitable" and mentally they were already "at War"; the "favourable opportunity" had to be awaited and it came with the assassination of the heir to the Emperor Francis Joseph.

In exactly the same way, the year 1926, and following years, are instrumental *in setting in motion that train of events* that *must* in the end produce War, although the worst features of it may be delayed for some years later.

It is ominous from an astrological standpoint that during 1926, and the following seven to eight years, certain combinations of the planets such as Mars and Saturn *will be extremely menacing.* This will cause unrest in all nations influenced in any way by Mars or Saturn, the fevered apprehensions that seem to force nations into provocative acts, the prelude to war described by Clauwitz as "the ideal atmosphere for preparations for conflict."

This combination of Mars and Saturn will more particularly affect the following nations: England, Germany, Japan, China, Macedonia, Russia, France, Italy, Roumania, Bohemia, Poland, Albania, Bulgaria, Greece, Mexico, India, Abyssinia, the Sudan, Rome as a City, Palestine, Syria, Damascus, Algeria, the Transvaal, South Africa and parts of Australia.

In all the countries and places mentioned the before mentioned combination of the planets Mars and Saturn will bring unrest among the people, revolutions and strikes, failure of crops, stringency of money, destruction of property, great fires, storms of unusual severity and earthquakes in many places that have in recent years been immune from such occurrences.

In countries more immediately influenced by Mars, such as England, Germany and Japan, devastating fires and explosions from seemingly unknown causes will occur in striking frequency. Earthquakes, earth subsidences, tidal waves and storms will also affect these countries, together with the fall of thunderbolts and meteorites of an unusual kind.

Gigantic sunspots and magnetic disturbances will upset climatic conditions in all countries from the year 1926 to the end of 1938.

Disasters by sea, storms, and earthquakes, will cause appalling loss of life and property in Japan, China and India.

China will especially be devastated by war, pestilence, floods and famine, and financial stringency.

India will have serious failures of crops, riots among the people, religious disturbances, and general upheaval.

France will experience one financial crisis after the other, unrest and dissatisfaction in her Army and Navy, continual changes of Government, plots, and dangers of revolution.

The trade of England prior to 1938 will be shaken to its foundations; her exports will shrink to their lowest ebb, unemployment will reach enormous figures, the country will pass through the severest crisis in her history and thousands of her workpeople will be reduced to starvation.

In foreign affairs she will receive terrible blows to her prestige. She will experience troubles in all her colonies and possessions, and will find the influence of Russia increasingly opposed to her in China, India, Persia, Afghanistan and Tibet.

In China, English trade will reach its lowest ebb, English property will be destroyed, English lives lost, and the menace of War in the Far East as well as in Europe will be extremely grave.

A treaty of the most far-reaching importance will be revealed during 1926 between Russia and a combination of interests antagonistic to Great Britain.[1] Almost at the same time the Bolshevick "Reds" will back up revolution in China, and will stimulate a similar movement in India and in all other countries.

Saturn, afflicting China with peculiar malignancy, will cause one upheaval after another. The Chinese will destroy Japanese, English, and American property. Soviet Russia will come to the assistance of the Chinese with immense quantities of war material, England and the United States will find themselves in the end forced against their wish to take drastic action, and the results will be far-reaching.

Japan, annoyed by the non-renewal of her former alliance with England, and the United States legislation against her nationals holding property in the States, will hold aloof from interference in China until the time comes *for her to act alone.* In the end she will come forward as the saviour of China, an alliance will be formed between the two countries and Japan and China will shake themselves free from all foreign interference in the Far East.

[1]A Treaty was made in March, 1926, between Soviet Russia and Germany.—[ED.]

From the end of 1926 and all through the following ten years strange combinations will be forming in Southern Europe in which Russia, Turkey, Bulgaria, Greece, Italy, Spain and France will be involved.

Turkey will become modernised in every way, and develop into a menacing Power in Asia Minor, Syria and Palestine. Italy, France, Greece, Bulgaria, Yugo-Slavia and Russia will be afflicted with "war fever," and a grave international crisis will be provoked. During the next few years France will be drawn into a dangerous position both at home and in Northern Africa and Syria; she will receive a severe blow to her prestige as a Colonial Power which will be followed by one crisis after another in Paris. A surprise will be caused by the concerted action of exiled Royal Families living in France, some form of revolution will be attempted and the country will be divided into three armed camps of Republicans, Royalists and Communists. Out of this turmoil a Dictator will in the end emerge and a new form of Government for the time being will save France.

Italy, during 1927, 1928, 1929, 1930, 1931 and 1932, will make many constitutional changes of the most dramatic nature. Several sensational trials will take place and a surprising move will be made with regard to the Vatican. This will lead to active hostility between the Government of Italy and the Church of Rome, and a situation will arise without precedent in any Catholic country. Italy will seize important positions in the Mediterranean and Africa and will hold them by force of arms. In this she will be aided by Spain, and to the astonishment of the world none of the Great Powers will oppose Italy's plan. Destructive earthquakes will do considerable damage during the next ten years in Italy, large towns will be destroyed, and some unusual phenomena will take place.

During these years Italy will enter on a remarkable era of success and power. She will become one of the most militant of the European nations, and will keep the War Cauldron for several years at fever-heat. She will become embroiled with Turkey and the Balkan States, and Russia will seize an opportunity of forcing the hand of Europe.

If this conflict should break out, England, and France, will endeavour to keep out of the carnage, but they will only be able to do so for a limited time. The danger again comes from that unknown and almost unknowable power—Russia.

The ignorance of Europe as a whole in connection with what they have always called "the Great Bear" is incomprehensible.

Since the time of the Saracen Invaders this vast Asiatic Empire has been regarded by one and all as some mystery land to be plundered or pillaged at the will of any adventurer who could find enough backing for the enterprise. An example may be taken of the disastrous attempt made by the great Napoleon in his march on Moscow. The appalling destruction of property, carnage, and loss of human life that followed did not teach European nations the lesson they might have learned. There is not a single country in Europe that has not attempted at some time or another to exploit the untold riches of Russia.

As if some mysterious Fate with jealous eyes watched to defeat scheme after scheme to bring away the Russian wealth, it has been one long history of wasted effort and useless endeavour.

Belgian financiers poured millions into Russian industries that came to nothing; France lent milliards, and then more milliards to get her first milliards back—all to no purpose.

The hard-headed English dreamt the dreams of Midas in forming Russian companies and opening up her mines, but their wealth has also been swallowed up.

But the reason you ask—what is the reason? Occultism is the only key that unlocks the mystery.

Away back in those long past ages when men studied nature and learned her secrets, Great Teachers in handing down the plan of the Heavens to following generations had for some unfathomable reason attributed to that vast country of Russia in the Zodiacal scheme of things the Sign of Aquarius with Saturn, its ruler, to be her symbol.

Mysterious and wonderful is it not in thinking over these matters to recollect that as in human lives Saturn is the dread planet of Fate, so in the destiny of nations this country which in her symbolism stands for Saturn must also play the same rôle in the history of the world.

In all forms of Occultism this mysterious planet—the last of what are called "the seven creative planets" of the earth's system—has been chosen to represent inexorable and relentless Destiny, the mysterious force which nothing can resist, that something which in all lives humbles the pride of the greatest and makes men realise the vanity of their pretensions.

In those marvellous pictures of Greek mythology Saturn is represented as the god who devours his own children.

Returning to Astrology for a further explanation, we find that the planet Saturn is placed as Lord or Ruler of the Zodiacal Sign of Aquarius.

Now the symbol of Aquarius is the "Water Bearer," a curious figure of an old man pouring water from a ewer upon the earth, and from this mysterious picture a mine of philosophy and wisdom may be explored.

Saturn may devour his own children, Time may bring into being—and destroy. The God who gave may also take away, but behind all is the Water Bearer pouring out water on the earth that in due course it may bring forth seed time and harvest, that men may sow and men may reap, that the eternal purpose of creation may in the end be carried out.

Let us try to grasp the hidden lesson which lies within the heart of this strange picture of Saturn as Lord of the Sign of Aquarius in its bearing on the future of Russia and her relation to the rôle she will be called upon to play in the Destiny of Nations.

Like the mythological god Saturn, Russia has destroyed her own children. Famine, plague and war have swept through this land over and over again. Peter the Great in his obstinate determination to build the city of St. Petersburg, now Leningrad, out of marshes on the borders of the Neva caused thousands of lives to be sacrificed. History relates that over a hundred men a day died in their efforts to drag the huge block of granite from far off mountains to its site in St. Petersburg to form the base of his statue.

Every few years, even to recent times, Russians caused "pogroms" to massacre Russian Jews by the thousand. In the Crimean War against Turkey, France and England, whole regiments of Russian soldiers were sent to their death, while in the Russo-Japanese War the loss of life could never be estimated. In the last Great War, Russia sacrificed more men than any other nation, and as if this was not enough, during the recent Bolshevick Revolution more men, women and children were destroyed *than in any other revolution that has ever been known*. All this has happened to a country whose Zodiacal ruler is the planet Saturn.

Let us now consider the hidden meaning that is conveyed in her sign in the heavens being that of Aquarius, the "Water Bearer." All down the ages the symbol of this sign has been that of an old man pouring water on the earth from a ewer he carries on his back.

There are two meanings given to this strange symbol, one the apparent contradiction of the other—just as the character of the Russian people on the whole is full of the wildest contradictions.

One of these meanings—the pouring out of the water—is that of wastefulness or prodigality; the other that of regeneration.

The day will come when the Russian waste of blood—the blood she has, and will yet pour out like water—will make "a new heaven and a new earth." The Day of Russia has not yet come!

When will it be? The answer is again given by the heavens.

By a knowledge of "the Precession of the Equinoxes" science teaches us that it takes 2,150 years for the Sun to retrograde through a single sign of the Zodiac. At the time when Abraham, the Father of the Hebrews, received "the promise" the Sun was in the Sign of Aries the Ram, and in its beautiful allegorical language, the Bible gives us the picture of Abraham saving his only son from the Altar of Sacrifice and offering up a Ram in his stead.

Two thousand one hundred and fifty years later, the Sun entered into the Sign of Pisces the Fishes, and another great epoch opened in the history of the world when Christ selected fishermen to be his disciples—to one of whom he promised he would make of him "a fisher of men." From that period which gave the dawn of Christianity, the fall of Jerusalem and the dispersal of the Jews, a definite milestone in history, 2,150 years has run its course and we have already commenced the period of the entry of the Sun into the Sign Aquarius when the mysterious Aquarian Age has commenced its dawn across the world, and already its first rays have revolutionised Russia, China, India, and countries that come under its influence.

A great leader of men will about this time appear. As this strange 2,150 year cycle is so intimately interwoven with the history of the Israelites, this Leader will unquestionably come from this race, and will in the end dominate Russia.

A new idea of Government will little by little spread from this country, which will completely revolutionise Europe, Asia, and the Far East, and Russia will become the most powerful nation in the history of modern civilisation.

The "old" is about to give birth to the "new." In all lands, in all peoples, the "travail pains" are becoming more and more intense. The last War was but "the turning in the womb" of Nature; the real birth has yet to come.

Alack and alas, to those who must cling to the "old"; to the traditions of the past, to the habits of their forebears;—their day has already passed forever.

The Clock of Time has struck the "Midnight Hour"; the blackest darkness lies before the greatest dawn.

The cry; "O Lord, how long,—how long?" will break from many hearts before the light of the new civilisation will chase away the shadows of the night.

During the coming years the influence of Communism will spread like an infective fever through all countries, the most fantastic doctrines will be openly preached and absorbed by all classes. Rich men will give away their wealth and gladly become poor; kings will break bread with workers and workers will dictate to kings; sons and daughters of the highest will become Socialists, and the lands they inherit they will give to the people.

Even "the Church" will have revolution within itself. Strange creeds will be preached from all pulpits.[1]

For a time Religion will save herself from catastrophe by abolishing her Bishops' "palaces," her gilded ceremonials, and her alliance with Monarchs. State and Church will separate and will cease backing up one another. Under the guise of humility Religion will creep back to her cradle of poverty and persecution, and in the next hundred years there will be as many religions sects in the World as there are pieces of the supposed "true Cross" in existence at the present time.

In the coming years, great evangelical "revivals" will sweep through all countries, side by side with Anarchy, Atheism, and Free Thought of every kind. Civilisation will chameleon-like change its colour to suit each wave of thought, and Chaos will drive her chariot of destruction through fields of Peace into the avenues of War.

[1]In the last few years schisms have destroyed the unity of "the Church of England," a new Prayer Book has been evolved and Bishops are at war with Bishops over the Communion Service.

It is only War in the end that will save humanity. It is only when the world will be satiated with blood, destruction and violence, that it will wake from its present nightmare of madness—and thus it is that the coming "War of Wars" fits into the design of things.

Through intense tribulation shall man be brought nearer to perfection and more fitted to enjoy the wonders of the new Aquarian Age, that, born in blood and sacrifice, will in the end fulfil the meaning of its symbol "the Water Bearer" whose pouring out of water on the earth is the emblem of unselfishness—the negation of Self—arrived at through suffering.

CHAPTER II

THE FATE OF NATIONS (*Contd.*)

THE BRITISH EMPIRE

I HAVE given a general outline of combinations of nations affecting the future of the British Empire in the immediate years. I would, however, be neglecting my duty if I did not give more specific information concerning the future—as I see it—of what is undoubtedly the greatest conglomeration of races that has up to now been brought into being.

I am only repeating a well-known truism by saying that no other Empire in the known history of the world has been as large, as powerful, or as diversified as that combination of races over which the Union Jack has flown.

As nothing exists without a cause I will try by the light of occultism to illuminate, be it ever so faintly, the mystery of the far off origin of the British Empire.

English history, as given to us in the ordinary way, has generally contented itself by stating that Britain was discovered by the Romans in 55 B.C. Who the previous inhabitants were has scarcely been touched upon, although it is on record that Cæsar stated that the inhabitants of the interior of Britain "were said by tradition to have sprung from the soil."

In some accounts we are briefly informed that the south-western coasts were known to the Phœnicians some centuries before the Christian era, and that they were attracted to Britain on account of its mines of tin.

History tells us that the Phœnicians were of Semitic origin, closely related to the Hebrews in language; but it also adds that they derived their name from the Phœnix, who was the emblem of the Phœnicians and from whom they took their name.

We are further told that the Phœnix was a symbol of the Sun, and that it was worshipped in ancient Egypt at the place called by the Greeks Heliopolis or by the Egyptians the "City of On," one of the names of the Sun.

Here on the very dawn of history we find the first gleam of light that leads our steps to the unknown shores of Britain. To the ancient Masters of Occultism it had become revealed that the days of "On," the City of the Sun of Egypt, were numbered.

To those world travellers, the Phœnicians, the order came to found another Centre that in symbolism would be worthy of the name of

"On" and emblematic of the Phœnix that rose again and again from its own ashes.

Thus it came about that ages before the Romans had heard of Britain, Phœnician mariners found their way up the Thames and founded a city to which they gave the name El-on-don, or the City of the Sun, a promise *in symbolism* that the city so named would become a centre, which, like the Sun, would radiate power, life and riches throughout the world.

Such, briefly, was the origin of London.

History tells us that when the Romans arrived in Britain in 55 B.C. "they found London a place of considerable importance, and that it had its own gold coinage."[1]

Let us now return to the Phœnicians. These early pioneers had brought with them the ancient religion of the Chaldeans, Egyptians and Hebrews. The foundation of these religions was "the wisdom of the heavens" or "the teaching *from* the heavens." At many places on the continent in their travels northward, and in various parts of Britain and especially at Stonehenge on Salisbury Plain they erected those mysterious monuments of huge stones which have been falsely attributed to the Druids. Recent discoveries have, however, proved that Stonehenge in those ancient times was a representation of the Zodiac

[1]Hume's *History of England.*

surrounding an Altar to the Sun of immense size.

That the long forgotten discoverers of Britain who took such trouble to convey these huge pillars of stone to Salisbury Plain, were well versed in Astronomical Science is exemplified even in our own day by the number of people who go every year to what is called the "hele stone" to see the Sun's rays at dawn on the 21st of June envelop this great pillar, just as those ancient people did so long ago that their very name and record have been forgotten, or lost in the dust of the centuries that have covered their footsteps.

Those ancient Students of the Heavens did even more than erect the great Temple at Stonehenge. In founding the City of London or El-on-don, as they called it, they placed it in the Zodiacal scheme of the universe as being governed by the Sign of Gemini, the Twins, and so there came down through the ages the legend of Gog and Magog as the gods who controlled the destiny of the great City they had established.[1]

Far back in the records of ancient astrology we find that the Ruler of the Sign of Gemini is the planet Mercury, the symbolism of which is commerce, business, finance, science and all such mental qualities. And so it was that even

[1]The names of Gog and Magog are intimately associated with the City of London even in our own day, and carvings representing them may be seen in various parts of the city.

in those far off days London became the centre or home of such things and has remained so all through the ages, until our own time.

As if to protect this jewel of mental symbolism, these ancient students, in the scheme of the Zodiac, placed the rest of England as governed by the warrior planet Mars in the Sign of Aries.

Mars is the symbol of iron, steel, machinery of all kinds, whether used for peace or war, and as the centuries evolved England became famous for her trade in iron, her machines and her engines of war.

In latter years Shakespeare alludes to this when he writes: "England thou seat of Mars."

The real origin of the Phœnicians is lost in antiquity, but there is every reason to believe that they had absorbed or were part of the "lost ten tribes" of Israel, who, fulfilling prophecies made centuries before, were "dispersed among the heathen," and who, in their wanderings northward, came and settled in Britain.

There are many legends which go to prove that the Phœnicians, and with them remnants of the "lost tribes," were the first settlers in Ireland. Many Irish towns and places derive the root word of their name from ancient Hebrew words. Long before the Saxon or the

Dane had been heard of, some of the most celebrated laws of Ireland appear to have been modelled on those given to the Children of Israel in the Book of Deuteronomy.

The famous Hill of Tara, from which the Irish Kings held their first Government and issued some of the wisest edicts that have ever been formulated, contains in the word "Tara" a Hebrew word which means "the law of the two tables."

Legend and history relate that about the year 580 B.C. King Heremon of Ireland was married to an eastern princess who was the daughter of Zedekiah, the last King of the House of Judah. It is said that this Princess with some other daughters of the Royal House of Judah escaped from the Babylonian captivity which history tells us took place about that same date. This escape of the daughters of the last King of Judah is very clearly recorded in the Book of Jeremiah, Chapter xliii, where it states that the King's daughters escaped "and came into the land of Egypt even to Tahpanhes," and history further informs us that at the Babylonian invasion of Egypt a "remnant of the House of Judah fled into other countries."

The Irish legend bears out in an extraordinary way the prophecy of Jeremiah that "the remnant that has escaped of the House of Judah shall again take root downward and bear fruit upward." It was in the natural order of things that King Zedekiah's daughter should make her way to Ireland, which country was well-known to Egyptian and Phœnician mariners, and this being so, it becomes equally natural to follow the legend, that this Princess of the House of Judah, with some of her people, brought with her to Ireland "the stone of Destiny" that Hebrew tradition states was the stone on which Jacob rested his head at Bethel when the blessing was given, that "thy seed shall spread abroad to the west, and to the east, and to the north, and to the south: and in thee and in thy seed shall all the families of the earth be blessed."[1]

Hebrew history relates that Jacob gave this stone which was his pillow to Joseph, that it was preserved through the Egyptian captivity, formed the seat of Solomon's Throne in Jerusalem, and is to-day the Coronation Stone on which every Englsih King is crowned since the far off days of Edward the First. The Irish and Scottish legends are still more explicit. The first relates that the stone was brought to King Heremon of Ireland by his marriage with the daughter of King Zedekiah, the last king of Judah, and that it was the Coronation Stone of the Irish Kings until Fergus O'Moore took it with him to Scotland when he became King of Argyll in A.D. 487. For more than 800 years

[1]Genesis xxviii, 14.

each King of Scotland was crowned on it until it was taken to London by Edward the First in 1298. Since then it has been used in the coronation of every English Monarch, with the sole exception of the Roman Catholic Queen Mary, down to the present King of England.

The following verse from the pen of Sir Walter Scott may well have an inspired meaning:

> "Unless the Fates have faithless grown,
> And prophet's voice be vain,
> Where'er is found this Sacred Stone,
> The wanderer's race shall reign."

It is not generally known, but I can personally vouch for it, that at the end of the Great War a secret society was formed in Ireland whose purpose was the smuggling out of England of this mysterious stone. This plot failed because the time was not ripe, but during the new Aquarian Age that is now breaking across the world I feel confident that the Stone of Destiny will be restored to the Israelites and will some day again be set up in the reconstructed City of Jerusalem.[1]

It is not my province to enter into the controversy as to whether the English and Ameri-

[1]Further remarks regarding "The Stone of Destiny" will be found in Part II, relating to Scotland.

cans are "the lost ten tribes" or not. An enormous amount of literature on this subject has been issued in recent years, and considerable evidence has been collected to prove that the two sons of Joseph, Ephraim and Manasseh, are to-day represented by England as the children of Ephraim and the U.S.A. as Manasseh. My own opinion is that such a proposition appears to limit the purpose of the Creator and brings too much into the controversy the personal element of the English and American people.

The design and purpose of "the Lord of Hosts" must be something so far beyond any personal bias or limitation that, in comparison, the destiny of even such great nations as the British and American fades into nothingness when regarded in the light of Divine Design as revealed in the histories of long past races.

Man is so apt to see things from his own petty point of view that he becomes carried away by a mistaken sense of his own importance. In the same way he too often regards the race he belongs to as superior to any other, or the God he worships as the only God which controls the universe.

The present so-called "Great Powers," in the intoxication of their youth, forget they are but children in comparison with races which have passed away. Five hundred years ago the British as a world nation were unknown;

Germans and French were equally unheard of, and the United States was still unborn.

With the innocence of children they prattle of their greatness, forgetting that before they uttered their first cry, the world had already trembled beneath the armies of Medes, Persians and Egyptians, and that Incas, Mayas, Astecs, and Hindus had civilisations beyond the wildest dreams of our imagination.

Blinded by vanity man too easily forgets the lessons of the past; the rise and fall of nations; the birth, youth, age and decay of races that existed long before his own had been called into being.

Returning to the supposition that the "lost ten tribes" of Israel, or at least some part of them, settled in Britain long before the Roman invasion, it is interesting to note that there are carvings on stones and monuments still existing that prove that settlements of Israelites coming from the Euphrates, flowed through the Crimea into Russia and spread northwards into far off countries. In the Crimea hundreds of gravestones have been recently found with Hebrew inscriptions and on one may be read, "Zadok, son of Moses, died 4,000 years after the Creation, 785 years after our exile." The exile thus referred to can be no other than the Assyrian captivity of the ten tribes which history relates took place about 720 B.C.

There is also plenty of evidence to prove that

about this time a strange race came out of the lands surrounding the Euphrates and spread northwards through Russia, Scandinavia, and Western Europe.

That this mass of people could be no other than the "lost tribes" of Israel is well supported by those words so full of meaning in the Second Book of Esdras, chapter xiii, verses 41, 42, where one reads "the ten tribes took this counsel among themselves that they should leave the multitude of the heathen and go forth into a far off country, *that they might keep their statutes, and they passed by way of the Euphrates.*"

In his history of Britain John Milton writes, "The Saxons were a people thought by good writers to be descended from the Sakai or Sacæ who with a flood of other nations came into Europe."[1] There is every reason to believe that these wandering races were first known as Sons of Isaac, bearing out as this does, the command of the twelfth verse of Genesis, twenty-first chapter, "In Isaac shall thy seed be called"; later they became Isaacsons and family Saxons. As the tribe of Dan came from the land of Jordan or Jor-*dan*, it is conceivable that they should have left traces of their name wherever they settled. This is borne out by the names they left behind in

[1]The ancient historian, Diodorus, also states that the Sacæ came from a race from Media, and Ptolemy mentions that the Saxons can be traced to a race called Sakai who came from Media.

their northward march, such as the *Dan*-ube, the *Dan*-iester, the *Dan*-etz, the *Dan*-dari, the *Dan*-ric Alps, and *Dan*-mark, later called Danemark. In ancient maps of Ireland one sees such names as *Dans*-lough, *Dan*-sower and *Dan*-gan which latter place became famous as the birthplace of Wellington.

Ten different Irish histories mention that a Hebrew teacher or prophet came to Ireland about the year 580 B.C. with the daughter of Zedekiah, the last King of Judah, and caused the famous Hall of Tara to be built. This Hebrew prophet was none other than Jeremiah whose medallion may still be seen carved in stone in the Courts of Justice in Dublin.

In Jeremiah, chapter xxxi, verse 21, one reads: "Set thee up waymarks, make thee high heaps: set thine heart toward the highway, even the way which thou wentest," and curious as it may seem, among the Irish there is a legend that *the strange round high mount* called the Hill of Tara was made by Jeremiah and contains the last Ark of the Covenant.

To many persons it may be a surprise to learn that the early inhabitants of Britain, especially those in Ireland, Scotland and Wales, used the Hebrew language extensively, and it is considered that upwards of forty per cent. of the English language is derived from the Hebrew. In fact, the great William Tyndale who translated the New Testament, wrote: "The Greek agrees more with the Englyshe than with the Latyne *but the properties of the Hebrew tongue agreeth a thousand times more* with the Englyshe than with the Latyne."

The origin of the word England is decidedly Hebrew. It is well known that the emblem of a Bull stood for the tribe of Joseph and his descendants; in Hebrew the word "bull" is "engl" or "angl" and so it is reasonable to suppose that when the descendants of Joseph came in those far off days into "the isles of the North," they called the new country they had entered "engl-land" which later became formed by use into the word "England." This is also the origin of the symbol "John Bull," which equally stands for Great Britain. The Unicorn, another of England's emblems, is a mixture of a horse and a bull—the head, the body and the legs are derived from the horse, while the feet, the tail and the horn, come from the bull, and it is instructive to remember that the ensign on the flag of Hengist, the Saxon, when he invaded Britain was a *white horse with the feet of a bull.* For confirmation of this I refer my readers to that well-known work on heraldry called "National Arms." Read also Deut., chapter xxxiii, verses 16-17: "Let the blessing come upon the head of Joseph, and upon the top of the head of him that was separated from his brethren. His glory is like the *firstling of his bullock*, and his horns are like the horns of unicorns."

There is yet another point that is of the deepest significance when considering the origin of England, namely, that the words Britain and British are also derived from a Hebrew-root, "Brith" meaning covenant and "ish" man. The Israelites were always known as the Covenant people, "the Covenant between God and his chosen race" being referred to again and again throughout the Bible.

It is not my province in a book of this kind to go more deeply into this side of the question of the connection between the "lost ten tribes of Israel" and the British race, but I think I have said enough to prove that there is a mysterious occult meaning and design underlying the origin of Great Britain, which will make itself still more manifest when we come to consider later the Armageddon in which Anglo-Saxons and Israelites will fight shoulder to shoulder to fulfil the prophecies made thousands of years ago as to the destiny of Palestine. There can be no doubt that the British Isles are referred to in many places in the Bible. In Isaiah, chapter xlix, verses 1, 3, and 6, we read:

"Listen, O isles, unto me; and hearken, ye people, from afar . . . . Thou art my servant, O Israel, in whom I will be glorified. It is a light thing that thou shouldest be my servant *to raise up the tribes of Jacob,* and *to restore the preserved of Israel.*"

Again in Isaiah, chapter lx, verse 9, one may read:

"Surely *the isles* shall wait for me, and the ships of Tarshish first, to bring thy sons from far, their silver and their gold with them."

The explanation of the word Tarshish can be found in Genesis, chapter x, verses 4-5, where, dealing with the descendants of Noah, it says "and the sons of Javan, Elishah, and *Tarshish,* Kittim and Dodanim. By these were *the isles of the Gentiles* divided in their lands."

The children of Tarshish eventually possessed the west coast of Europe and that name may still be found in ancient maps. This part embraced that region now called Spain, Portugal, France and "the isles" of Britain. On some old maps Britain is called Javan. In Genesis, chapter x, verse 2, we are told that Javan was one of the descendants of Japheth, Noah's third son. Other references to the children of Tarshish and Javan are equally interesting and support my former statement that Britain was known and inhabited by the Phœnicians and Israelites long before the Roman invasion. In 2 Chron., chapter ix, verse 21, speaking of the reign of Solomon it states:

"For the King's ships went to Tarshish with the servants of Huram: every three years once came the ships of Tarshish bringing gold, and silver."

In the twenty-seventh chapter of Ezek., verse 12, we read:

"Tarshish was thy merchant by reason of the multitude of all kinds of riches; with silver, iron, tin, and lead, they traded in thy fairs," and verse 19: "Dan also and Javan going to and fro occupied in thy fairs."

Tarshish and Javan are also mentioned as a refuge for those who escaped from the captivity of the Assyrians. In the sixty-sixth chapter of Isaiah, verse 19, we read:

"And I will set a sign among them, and I will send those that escape of them unto the nations, to *Tarshish*, Pul and Lud . . . to Tubal *and Javan* to *the isles afar off*, that have not heard my fame, and they shall declare my glory among the Gentiles."

It is therefore evident that the average histories describing the Britons at the time of the Roman invasion A.D. 55 as half-savage barbarians, are decidedly wrong, for even in the time of Solomon merchants from Javan traded to far off countries with ships carrying "silver, iron, tin and lead."

Sir Edward Cressey in his History of England writes:

"The British tin mines mainly supplied the glorious adornment of Solomon's temple."

Homer, who lived about 800 B.C., in Book xviii describes the smelting foundries of Tarshish, also the coats of mail made in ancient Britain wrought "with gold and brass and tin." In fact civilisation in "the isles" of Britain and Ireland was far in advance of any neighbouring country long before the Legions of Rome marched through Gaul.

The Greek philosopher Pliny wrote "The whole of the Empire of Rome was supplied with tin and metals from Britain." He also says that Greece was furnished with tin and various metals from Britain as far back as 907 B.C.

Aristotle (380 B.C.) mentions the British Islands by their names, "Beyond the Pillars of Hercules the ocean flows round the earth, in this ocean are Islands called Britannic, Albion and Ierne (Ireland)."

Strabo who was born about 60 B.C. tells a story of a Phœnician Captain who destroyed another ship so as to prevent her sailors finding out where the isles of Tarshish lay.

All this simply goes to prove how much more ancient British civilisation is than most people have any idea of.

How many people who have gazed upward at the dome of St. Paul's Cathedral have dreamt for a moment that it stands on the foundations of a Pagan Temple erected by the Phœnicians to the Sun-God in some age long before the dawn of Christianity had appeared.

These wonderful Phœnician sailors were far from being ignorant. In 616 B.C. history tells us they sailed out of the Red Sea round the entire coast of Africa and returned to Egypt through the Straits of Gibraltar *twenty-one centuries before* Vasco de Gama discovered the Cape of Good Hope in 1497.

It is believed that the Phœnicians with "the escaped of Israel" came to Britain about the time of the capture of Jerusalem by the Assyrians (780–760 B.C.). This date tallies with the "dispersal of the lost ten tribes among the heathen" and accounts in a great measure for the mixture of Pagan and Hebrew religion that we still find traces of in London.

As I said earlier in this book it was the Phœnicians who gave the name to this City of El-on-don—in symbolism the City of the Sun as prophetic of its future glory and position in the world of men. On the highest part of this city, these ancient Phœnicians in their wonderful knowledge of Astrology built a Temple to the Sun in the Sign of Gemini otherwise called "The Twins," or Gog and Magog, which from most ancient times has been considered as the Sign of the Zodiac which rules London. Even to-day on the western pediment of this great church, now called St. Paul's Cathedral, the emblematical figures of the four divisions of the Zodiac as Spring, Summer, Autumn and Winter may be seen, while on the top of this pediment there is a hieroglyphical representation of the Sun in its highest point in the heavens, namely, when it enters the constellation of the Sign of Gemini. From this exalted position his beams of glory appear to be striking a man from a horse, which gives the astrological meaning that the Sun in that position of the Zodiac is in opposition to the Centaur or half-man-half-horse of the constellation of Sagittarius in December, the exact opposite Sign of the Zodiac to that of Gemini. This great edifice, dedicated to "The Twins" by the ancient Phœnicians and later called Castor and Pollux by the Greeks, *considered the greatest of all the gods,* bore in later years the designation of the Temple of Pollux; from that it became abbreviated to the Temple of Pol and when England became Christianised its name easily passed to the church of Paul and later still the Cathedral of Saint Paul.

Those who do not think imagine that the allegorical carving I call attention to represents the conversion of Saint Paul, but if they do, they forget that in the story of the conversion there is no mention of any horse. On the contrary, we are told that when Paul got on his feet "he was led by the hand by those who were with him."[1]

The form of swearing, Per Ædam Pollucis —by Pol's Cathedral—shows there was something out of the common in the size and grandeur of "Pol's Cathedral," but to the eyes of its original creators it had a still greater meaning and one more in keeping with the greatness of the city that they foresaw in later years would be built round it. It was not only that the original Gog and Magog, who were later called Castor and Pollux, were the greatest of all the gods, but they were considered *the guardians of property, the genius of banking security* and *wealth,* which was decidedly appropriate for the great Cathedral of London.

Let us now pass through this great building from the north to the south entrance, and there high up on the pediment one may see the form of Hercules which in ancient times stood for the masculine nature of the Sun. Here he represents a man holding a Saltire Cross which is a cross in the shape of an X, a goniometer or double pair of compasses showing the exact angle made by the Sun at his two crossings of the Equator in that far distant age when the worship of the Sun was first instituted. The angle indicated by this cross being now about 23° 28′ compared to what it was when noted by Ptolemy, is gradually decreas-

[1]Acts ix, 8.

ing at the rate of one minute per hundred years, consequently in about one hundred and forty thousand years from now this cross *will be completely closed*—the Ecliptic will then coincide with the Equator and there will be an equal length of day and night in all the earth and all the year round, *lasting for a thousand years* from which knowledge may have originated the idea of the promised millennium.

This figure of a man in the guise of the giant Hercules may be observed with the cross or measure of the Sun's angle behind his back—a symbol of the crucifixion of man. A sermon in stone handed down to humanity from a long past race whom in our wisdom (?) we are pleased to call—pagan.

How these ancient ideas were transmitted to us through the ages or were resurrected and incorporated in the rebuilding of St. Paul's Cathedral, may never be known, but one point that stands out in strange significance is the fact that its famous architect, Sir Christopher Wren, six years before he was requested by Charles II to submit plans for the restoration of St. Paul's, was a *Professor of Astronomy* at Oxford, and consequently was well versed in the older science of Astrology. It is also a curious fact that he chose the date of the 21st of June, 1675, to lay the first stone of the new Cathedral, which date is the Zodiacal Sign of the Twins, or Castor and Pollux, the same gods to whom the ancient Phœnicians dedicated their pagan Temple of Gog and Magog, and which Zodiacal sign had been given to London as its ruler and has remained so ever since.

History records that Wren as a young man had a close friend in Sir Isaac Newton and the latter was deeply versed in Astrology before he took up Astronomy. At nineteen years of age Newton himself tells us he had bought a book on Astrology. It is therefore probable that Wren in this way knew a great deal about the astrological ideas of the ancients and so incorporated them in his designs for the reconstruction of the Cathedral.

If still more examples are required of the knowledge and wisdom of the ancient inhabitants of Britain, I must ask my readers to accompany me to what is called "The Temple," opposite the Law Courts, and wander for a moment in the quiet atmosphere of its shady walks.

Why was this part of London called "The Temple" one naturally asks? The answer is given by observation of some of those carvings found over the arches of many of the buildings within the confines of its old world squares.

It may surprise some of my readers to hear that the original meaning of the Latin word "Templum" never had any bearing on any church, chapel or temple within the confines of this place. Many may be still more surprised when I demonstrate that its purpose, as planned by its long dead builders, *was the same as that for which it is employed to-day*, namely, *a place set apart where Law and Justice would be studied and administered.*

Words may alter their meaning and significance, but pictures expressed in symbolism speak the same language and carry their message down the centuries when those who carved them are completely forgotten.

Perhaps you have not noticed that over the main entrance, in the Strand, cut out in stone, is a clearly chiselled figure of a Lamb with a cross resting on its shoulder. You most probably thought when you first noticed this strange carving that it had some reference to Christ as the crucified Lamb. You may have wondered why such an emblem was erected in a place set apart for Law, and your wonder may have been still more increased when you found the same symbol on several other buildings within these precincts. In the end it is quite likely that you came to the conclusion that the emblem of a Lamb with a cross on its shoulder, might have been put there as a symbol of patience, meekness, and resignation—the required qualities necessary for those who invoke the aid of the Law.

Perhaps, in admitting that the Lamb was a suitable sign for such a place, you have puzzled over the meaning of the cross—and such an important-looking one at that. If you have had any experience of what Shakespeare calls "the Law's delays," you may have leapt to the conclusion that its meaning in such a place must have been to warn people of the mental, if not physical, crucifixion all must undergo if Justice has to be invoked. In your desire to know that you have solved the correct answer, you may, in a moment of impetuosity, have stopped some black-robed disciple of the Law and begged him for an explanation. If he was a briefless barrister—and such curiosities do exist in "the Temple"—he may have had the courtesy to reply, but if he did so, he, whether briefless or not, would probably have astonished you still more by admitting he had never noticed the carvings you referred to, or if he had, he most probably would answer that such things had something to do with Christianity, and as quickly pass on for fear he might show his ignorance still further.

Will it surprise you to hear that this curious carving of a Lamb and a Cross has nothing whatever to do with the Christian religion and that it was designed and employed centuries before the Cross became a religious emblem? [1] It is, in fact, purely an astrological symbol which can be traced back to the early Phœni-

[1] The Cross only became an emblem of Christianity when the Emperor Constantine made it so in the fourth century, and it was not included in Clement of Alexandra's Christian symbols.

cians. It represents the Lamb of Life when the Sun at the beginning of the Vernal Equinox *crosses* the Equator; in other words it is the "Passover" or "cross-over." It fixed the period of the year when the Israelites held their feast of the Passover and the month they called "the beginning of months." In those far distant ages the vernal equinox commenced in the Sign of Aries the Ram, the House of Mars. From the perfect equity of the Sun in its relation to the earth at this period of the year, giving as it does *equal length of day and night to all the world*, it became the symbol of equity, law, justice and judgment between men. It is therefore logical to find this emblem in a place set apart for the study of law, and erected there by that remarkable race whose traces in Britain date back to the very confines of history.

Such is the origin of what is called "the Temple" in the middle of London opposite the High Courts of Justice.

CHAPTER III

THE HOUSE OF WINDSOR AND ITS DESTINY

KING GEORGE V, QUEEN MARY, AND THE ROYAL FAMILY OF GREAT BRITAIN

The name of the Royal House of Hanover was altered by Royal Proclamation in London on July 17th, 1917, to that of THE HOUSE OF WINDSOR. *The change was made under unfavourable aspects of Saturn and Mars, a distinctly unfortunate time to choose for the alteration. In reading this chapter on the Royal Family of England, this should be borne in mind.*

WHAT does Fate hold for King George the Fifth and Queen Mary, and especially for that general favourite, the Prince of Wales, Heir-Apparent to the Throne of the British Empire?

If, as I have shown, the Future seems menacing for Europe, and the storm clouds are likely to again rain red with blood, what of the Monarch whose reign has been filled with anxieties and the greatest war England has ever known, in striking contrast with the placid days of Victoria and the pleasure-filled epoch of Edward the Seventh?

There can be no question that "the Sailor King," born as he was, with the planet Neptune rising at his birth, has earned the affection of his People. Moreover, peculiar interest centres upon his Heir, whose advancing years find him yet a bachelor, thereby setting up a precedent in the history of near heirs to the Crown of England; for a table of those who have borne the illustrious name of Prince of Wales reveals no bachelor after the age of twenty-five. At the present time the widespread impression gaining ground that the present Prince of Wales has no taste for the wearing of a crown has fixed increasing interest upon the studious attention of his brother, the Duke of York, to the exacting duties of the life ceremonial.

In all ages Kings and Princes have been closely connected with the researches of astrology and occultism. For their own enlightenment they maintained "Seers" and Astrologers; while it was a popular idea, and one not devoid of truth, that the planets in their courses told their own tale of events affecting the wearers of the Purple. Shakespeare voiced this when he wrote:

"*The Stars blaze forth the death of Princes.*"

Queen Anne, the last English monarch to maintain an astrologer upon the roll of the

Privy Purse, reposed such faith in the celebrated Von Galgebrok, the Dutch magician who dominated her court, that she desired him to predict the year of her death. He did so with perfect accuracy *three years before the event*, which took place on 1st August, 1714.

Let us now consider the astrological influences affecting the House of Windsor. Some of them are doubtful while others, I fear, are distinctly menacing.

Before entering into particulars, let me explain the astrological influences that swayed the destiny of Great Britain in the opening days of the War.

King George V. was born in London, on June 3rd, 1865, the sun being, at his date of birth, in the Sign of Gemini.

Queen Mary, his Consort, was born at White Lodge, near London, on May 26th, 1867, with the Sun also in the Sign of Gemini.

The Prince of Wales, Heir-Apparent, was born at Sheen, Richmond, London, June 23rd, 1894, on the "cusp" of the Sign of Gemini, the Sun being only 2.21 of the next Zodiacal Sign of Cancer.

Lord Kitchener, regarded as the chief military counsellor of the Government during the Great War, was born June 24th, 1850, also on the "cusp" of Gemini-Cancer the same sign.

In considering the astrological influences that overshadow King George and his House, I must record the remarkable occult history connected with the Hanoverian dynasty, as his House was called before the change was made by Royal Proclamation on July 17, 1917, which, in my judgment, was made on a day when the astrological influences were most unfavourable.

George the First, a Hanoverian Monarch, married his lovely young cousin, the Duchess of Zell in her own right. Her *liaison* with the romantic European adventurer, Count Konigsmark, is a classic of mystery and romance; on the eve of the projected elopement with the *debonair* Count, the Duchess was seized by her husband's servants and immured in the Castle of Ahlen, where she remained *for thirty-two years.* Meantime George obtained a divorce and commenced his reign as King of England and at the same time assumed the crown of Hanover.

The unhappy Duchess made a number of attempts to regain her liberty. She enlisted the help of the celebrated astrologer, Pard Zepl, a mysterious and cosmopolitan character who claimed to be a reincarnation of Alexander the Great. This Enigma formed a passionate attachment to the imprisoned Duchess. He cast a horoscope of King George the First, a document preserved for years in the Royal muniment vault of the ancestral home of the Hanoverian monarchs in Hanover. He predicted that the King would die *a year and a day after the Duchess.* She died 10th June, 1726; *on* 11*th June,* 1727, *George the First expired* in his carriage while entering his Hanoverian domain on one of his many visits.

It is remarkable how the period of April to July is bound up in the destiny of the present Royal Family of England. Events of supreme importance take place in the period April to 31st July for King George the Fifth, the Prince of Wales and other members of the Royal Family. In the same sense, this same period was equally significant for King Edward, as I explained to him when conversing on Occultism in his library at Marlborough House, before he came to the Throne.[1]

In the horoscope of King George the Fifth, the Trident, or Sign of the planet Neptune, is in the "rising sign" at the point of birth. This denotes that his natural bent was towards the ocean and a sailor's life; it illustrates how natural is his bluff and hearty manner com-

[1]George I died 11th June.
George III born 4th June.
Queen Charlotte born 7th June.
Queen Victoria born 24th May.
H.R.H. The Duke of York 3rd June.
H.R.H. Princess Mary of Teck May 26th.
H.R.H. Prince Edward June 23rd.
etc., etc.

mented upon recently by Colonel House in his intimate letters; he is rightly called "The Sailor King" as was his ancestor, his great-great Uncle, William the Fourth, also born under the planet Neptune.

In King George's horoscope, the Regal sign of the planet Jupiter is almost in mid-heaven in the Ninth House, and in a powerful position to Aries the Zodiacal Sign governing England. Thus, even when he was a sailor and a second son—with no expectation that he would come to the Throne as his brother the Duke of Clarence had every right to expect to reign—the promise of the planets was, that he should have Regal position and be destined to wear a Crown.[1] Mars is King George the Fifth's ruling planet in the House of Aries (England's Sign). From these astrological influences he received kingship and the natural dignity that well becomes him as a Monarch.

But the position of Saturn must be considered, it is disquieting and threatening all through his reign especially when one realises that this planet governs Russia in its Zodiacal Sign, as I have explained on page 38.

[1]Queen Victoria ascended the Throne 20th June.
Battle of Waterloo 18th June.
George II ascended the Throne 11th June.
William IV ascended the Throne 26th June.
King Edward VII died 6th May, 1910.
King George V succeeded to the Throne 6th May, 1910.
George V married 6th July, 1893.
Crowned at Westminster Abbey 22nd June, 1911.
Germany signed Peace Treaty 28th June, 1919.

The influence of this planet is unfavourable to King George and also to Aries, the Zodiacal Sign of England. Saturn is malignant in aspect, and baleful with increasing force as we enter into 1926 and the immediate following years. It promises unrest among the people, great and disastrous strikes, bad and restricted trade conditions, gathering clouds of war in countries more directly influenced by it, such as India, China, and Russia, and for the King himself it promises trials and anxieties that must in the end seriously affect his physical condition, especially the nerves, stomach and digestive organs.

The planetary influences governing King George will be unfavourable for him personally between 1928 and 1930.[1] I foresee in those years a critical time and a period of deep anxiety for the Royal Family and for the British Empire as a whole. This will be a period when His Majesty will be peculiarly exposed to danger of illness and accidents of all kinds, especially those caused by or from the air.[2] These portents are strange and ominous and full of meaning for the entire Empire, but still more directly for London, *placed as it is under Gemini the first House of Air.*

[1]The King's severe illness commenced in November, 1928, and lasted until the summer of 1930.

[2]The King's lungs were stricken with inflammation and pneumonia and several operations took place in order to drain the lungs of poison.

All through the years 1927, 1928, 1929 to 1932, the portents are not favourable for the prosperity of England or for the Royal Family, with the exception of the Duke of York. In his case, it is remarkable that the regal sign of Jupiter increases in power as the years advance, which, as I have explained, was also the case of his Royal father, before there was any likelihood of his coming to the Throne.

Not only King George, but Queen Mary also, comes under a combination of adverse influences. Nor does the Prince of Wales escape these falling shadows. His astrological chart shows perplexing and baffling influences that most unquestionably point to changes likely to take place greatly affecting the Throne of England.

The birth date of the Prince places him in a category of individuals who are strangely baffling in temperament. In the case of those who live ordinary lives, these peculiarities escape much comment or have little effect; but where it is a Prince of the Blood, called by birth to fill a high position it is a very different matter.

The Prince was born under peculiar astrological combinations which make his character a difficult one to understand. His planetary signs give intense restlessness, a lack of continuity of thought, a difficulty of concentration, and an absorbing love for change of scene and travel, and a lack of what may be called "a sense of danger." Physically there will be found a nervousness expressed by restless movements and lack of repose, as in a person "for ever on the move." Such individuals are apparently wildly changeable and are often accused of being insincere. But as a matter of fact they simply are dominated by different moods—hence their apparent chameleon character.

The Prince of Wales in his signs parallels in a strange fashion his ancestral namesake, George, Prince of Wales, afterwards Regent, and reigning as George the Fourth, "the First Gentleman of Europe." His disregard for Court ceremonial caused estrangement from his father, George the Third; his restless mind found an outlet in travel and exotic building schemes; his changeable ways were at once the despair and exasperation of his Ministers; yet he had a wonderful knack of catching and holding popular love. His relations with the fair sex remain to this day somewhat of a mystery.

That George the Fourth, when Prince, married Mrs. Fitzherbert, is supported by historical documents; the match was dissolved by an Act of Parliament which limited Royal Princes to ladies born within the "circle of Royal blood," and his subsequent marriage to

Caroline of Brunswick was a disaster culminating in her attempt to force her way into the Abbey of Westminster for a coronation denied her. Henceforth, George the Fourth "regarded women as mere playthings of an idle hour, but shuddered away from serious intimacy" according to Crevy, the Royal Gossip.

The present Prince of Wales has piqued curiosity many times by rumours of marriages that have faded away into the air. Even before the War, when he was a mere youth, he was affianced by rumour to a German Princess, one of the Schleswig-Holstein family. I said at that time that the astrological indications for the Prince put marriage practically into the background.

Since then Princesses from Italy, Russia, Sweden, Norway, Bulgaria and Greece have been confidently spoken of as future Princesses of Wales. Rumour says that Queen Mary, and in a lesser degree, King George, have worried themselves seriously over this problem of the Prince who may be fond of a light flirtation with the fair sex but is determined not to "settle down" until he feels a *grande passion*, but it is well within the range of possibility, owing to the peculiar planetary influences to which he is subjected, that he will in the end fall a victim of a devastating love affair. If he does, I predict that the Prince will give up everything, even the chance of being crowned, rather than lose the object of his affection. As of course, the Royal Marriage Act severely limits his choice, consideration having to be given to the question of the religion, birth, and even physical condition of the selected bride.

Born as he was in that part of the month of June that makes a peculiar period for astrological calculations (June 23rd, 1894), the Prince may be trusted to have decided views on love, and also will present the characteristics of apparent change that are baffling to those who cannot understand the significance of seeming alternations of "hot" and "cold." For persons born under such peculiar astrological conditions exhibit remarkable fluctuations of feeling—they pass from ardour to indifference almost in a few seconds, and they are very liable to be charged with inconstancy.

It is instructive that the astrological aspects of the Prince of Wales agree in the main with those of four of the sons of George the Third, and each of them baffled and bewildered the country by their inability to marry "sensibly" —that is, from a Court and dynastic point of view.

I have already dealt with the "love affairs" of the eldest son of George the Third. The Duke of Clarence, who later reigned as William the Fourth, lived for many years with Mrs. Jordan the actress, and by her had a large family. His proposal to Miss Wykeham, who rejected him, made a sensation.

The Duke of Kent, the next son, contracted an irregular alliance with Lady Augusta Murray, but the Royal Act dissolved this. Then he espoused, by another left-handed alliance, Lady Cecilia Buggin, and this union was also dissolved. He lived for years with a Madame Laurent, and was sixty when he was induced under pressure to give her up to marry the Princess Saxe-Coburg, whose child, born in Kensington Palace, May 24th, 1819, was destined to be Queen Victoria.

His Royal Highness Prince Henry, born March 31st, 1900, will have an eventful, but not a peaceful life. He will take an active interest in Military affairs and will have great danger in War. He is likely to be severely injured by fire, firearms and explosions, but an Army career will be the best for him to follow.

He will suffer from troubles in the throat, nose and ears, from bruises and breaking of the bones, especially the arms and shoulders.

His Royal Highness, Prince George, born December 20th, 1902, will fill high civil appointments such as those of Viceroy or Governor of Colonics. He will travel extensively and have many voyages, but the Sea as a profession would be unfavourable to him and also dangerous. In health he will have trouble with the stomach and internal organs, also with the feet and the upper part of the head.

Viewing the future, I see great and menacing times overshadowing England, while over the Palace of King George and the Royal Family, the immediate present and the coming years are full of ominous signs that have no parallel in recent times.

CHAPTER IV

THE BRITISH EMPIRE IN ITS WORLD ASPECT

THE LOSS OF THE WORDS "UNITED KINGDOM" PREDICTIONS REGARDING CHINA, INDIA, SOUTH AFRICA, AUSTRALIA, NEW ZEALAND AND CANADA

THE words "United Kingdom" which have recently been dropped out of the Imperial title of King George the Fifth have a remarkable occult meaning of their own.

This title came into existence in 1801 through the union of Great Britain and Ireland, and strangely enough must now disappear *by the admission of Ireland to the status of a Dominion.*

The words "United Kingdom" were added to the Imperial title in the reign of George the Third who was born in the same period of the Zodiac as the present King George the Fifth, namely, in what is known as the Sign of Gemini. Under the reign of George the Third, England lost her American Colonies, and in the reign of George the Fifth she lost Ireland.

These two words "United Kingdom" translated into numbers by means of the Mystic Alphabet [1] produce the total of fifty-one for the compound number and six for the single digit. In my *Book of Numbers* I have explained how important and powerful these numbers are. I have also illustrated how the compound numbers represent *the hidden forces that play on the destiny of persons or things*, whilst the single numbers represent the more material or visible state of existence.

The meaning of the symbolism of the Number 51, which as I said previously is the compound number of the words "United Kingdom," has a very striking significance with the history of England since the year 1801 when these two words first made their appearance as part of the Imperial title.

What I have published in my *Book of Numbers* about this number is as follows:

"This number has a very powerful potency of its own. *It represents the nature of the warrior*; it promises sudden advancement in whatever one undertakes; it is especially favourable for those in military or naval life and for leaders in any cause."

If such description had been specially made it could not better express the great destiny which followed the United Kingdom from 1801 to the present time.

[1] See Cheiro's *Book of Numbers*.

To those who are versed in the interpretation of signs and symbols the erasing of these magic words from the Imperial title of Great Britain conveys an extremely ominous significance.

The Ministers and advisors of His Majesty, who after all are but playthings in the hands of Destiny, have in their ignorance and in order to pander to the wishes of the representatives of the Irish Free State and the Colonies, drifted with that mysterious tide of things which is causing changes in dynasties and nations in every part of the world.

The Press in America and on the Continent have been quick to realise that important results are likely to follow the open avowal that "the United Kingdom" no longer exists. Many of the leading papers in the States have not hesitated to call this change as "the beginning of the breaking up of the British Empire."

The same occult influences which caused the Government of George the Third to lose the American Colonies have caused recent Governments of George the Fifth to withdraw British troops from Egypt, to grant India her own Navy, to abandon Ireland and to drop the magic words "United Kingdom" from the Imperial designation.

There is also an ominous meaning in the fact that this title was dropped in a period of the year that in the symbolism of the Zodiac is in *opposition to England,* and the same ominous signs were in operation at the conclusion of the Treaty between the Sinn Fein party which caused Southern Ireland to become "the Irish Free State" and which now, owing to Ireland being admitted into the status of a Dominion, is the actual cause of the alteration in the Imperial title and the new law which has made each Dominion master of its own destiny.

Since the Armistice in 1918 the planetary and occult influences governing the British Government, and the principal members of the Royal Family are what may be described as "giving" or "yielding" influences.

This is borne out by the continual giving way of every Government that has come into power since 1918 to any show of opposition that has cropped up. A few illustrations will be sufficient to show what I mean; submission to the United States' terms of payment for the War debts; non-renewal of the alliance with Japan in obedience to America's wishes; forgiveness of war debts from other nations; giving in to Northern Ireland's demand for a Parliament, followed by surrender to Sinn Fein; Egyptian Independence, a native Navy for India, industrial upheaval, and reduction of the Army and Navy, of Great Britain.

These ominous and destructive influences

must, I regret to say, continue until a crisis will arise in the history of the once called "United Kingdom" which will be greater than anything before experienced in its remarkable history.

Strange and unexpected changes will make themselves manifest during the years 1928, 1929 and 1930, concerning the relations between the British Colonies and the Mother Country.

A new Political Party will be formed in South Africa that will develop a hostile and aggressive policy against England, and commercial treaties and agreements will be made with other countries that will cause severe loss to British Trade.

A somewhat similar movement will spread through Australia and New Zealand, but in Australia the results will be extremely serious and the "Red" or Bolshevick element will become alarmingly active.

Owing to the overwhelming numbers of American films in comparison to British that are being shown in Cinemas and Theatres all over the Colonies, the propaganda for all things American will materially decrease the demand for British goods and the export trade from English ports will suffer accordingly.

During 1928 [1] a measure to deal with this question will be actively brought before Parlia-

[1] This took place.

ment and a large sum of money will be voted to subsidise the manufacture of English films in England. Owing to climatic conditions and lack of a fixed policy, this effort will more or less fail and many British film companies will be forced into liquidation.

Extraordinary unconventional and, in many cases, revolutionary changes will take place during 1928, 1929, 1930 and 1931 in connection with Parliament. Socialism and the Labour Party will make rapid strides and the Bolshevick menace will become still more acute.

A strike of far-reaching importance will be threatened during the early part of 1928 by transport and railway workers, but unusual methods adopted by the Government will prevent this danger coming to a head.

Owing to falling revenue a new system of taxation will be brought forward which will lead to opposition and disturbances all over Great Britain.

Trouble in India will loom large during 1928 1929, 1930, 1931, and many of the most powerful of the Maharajahs will become dissatisfied with British rule in that country. Serious riots and meetings will break out in many parts of India, especially Burmah, and all English possessions in the Far East will be menaced by bloodshed and rebellion.[1]

[1] This took place in Ghandi's opposition to the Government's Salt Monopoly.

Canada will be the one bright spot in the British Empire. Industry and trade will grow rapidly from East to West. American money will every year more and more develop Canadian industries. A working commercial agreement of far reaching importance will be made between the United States and Canada. Frontier restrictions will be so reduced that travel and trade between the two countries will be enormously increased.

During the next few years a scheme of colossal magnitude will be brought to fruition by the Railway and Shipping Magnates of Canada and the United States in the creation of a waterway to open up the lakes and rivers of Northern America, and bring ocean carrying ships from East to West across that great Continent.[1]

[1] This is already becoming fulfilled in the negotiations recently opened up between the Governments of Canada and the United States.

Chapter V

THE ORIGIN OF THE UNITED STATES AND ITS FUTURE ADVANCEMENT

THE OCCULT MEANING OF ITS HERALDIC SIGNS

THAT great Nation known as the United States of America, came into existence on the 4th July, 1776. All through the previous month of June negotiations for such a remarkable event as the "birth of a nation" were being concluded, the Continental Conference had met in Philadelphia and the Declaration of Independence had been agreed on. All this took place in strict accordance with the fact that for ages past it had been established by ancient Masters of Astrology and Occultism that the Sign of the Zodiac governing the United States, or in those days, that part of the Universe in which North America was finally discovered, was the House or Sign of Gemini, otherwise called "the House of the Twins," and the first House of Air. From a very old book in my possession, which contains astrological tablets copied from ancient manuscripts, it is interesting to quote what in those far off days, long before the Continent of America was discovered, were the qualities represented by the Sign of Gemini, which are extremely descriptive of the people of the United States taken as a whole. "This Sign of the heavens produces persons in stature lithe, lanky, active and energetic, generally of a sallow complexion, quick sighted piercing eyes, with a smart active look, dark or brown hair, rather thin, highly-strung nervous people, restless and always in motion, never satisfied, always building, rebuilding, constructing and reconstructing. Mentally this Sign of the heavens produces persons of keen intellects endowed with more invention and genius than any other sign of the Zodiac."

The Sign of Gemini has the planet Mercury as its ruler in its *positive or strongest aspect*, and again from the same authorities the following is a description of the qualities given to people born under this planet. "The mind is strong, vigorous, active, searching, exhausting both worlds and imagining new, the memory retentive, and tenacious, inheriting a natural thirst for knowledge which all the wells of discovered science cannot slake, but still does the intellectual soul wish ardent and aspiring for store after store of philosophic, classic, or celestial learning; generally the most eloquent orators, the most skilful philosophers, the most eminent mathematicians, and the most rare and curious of mankind are under the influence of this planet. In appearance the true type is that of a tall, upright, lanky, spare body, long nose, long visage, dark eyes, dark hair, thin legs and arms with long rather bony hands."

If the above descriptions had been specially written they could not more clearly describe the symbolic figure of "Uncle Sam" as he is generally depicted, and yet we must remember all that was compiled by the ancient Astrologers many thousand of years before the birth of Christ.

We will now consider the meaning of the Heraldic symbolism of nations especially that of the United States, which throws a wonderful and illuminating light on that mysterious Destiny of countries which is both interesting and instructive.

It is impossible to say definitely how or when the heraldic signs that have become so intimately associated with nations had their origin. There are some that no doubt have been slowly created by the ancient history of the country or land they represent, while others are of a more occult or mysterious origin, but one and all were thought out and created with some definite purpose and meaning, sometimes veiled or concealed by symbolism, and oftimes translated and explained by it—*and by it alone.*

One remarkable example of this is that proud emblem of France under the Monarchy—the Fleur de Lys. Ancient tapestries found in the Cathedral of Rheims explain its origin, which may surprise many people to hear was a very lowly one. It appears that in the early days of French history the conquering army that produced the first dynasty of Kings, coming from tracts in the centre of France where frogs were most numerous and not having perhaps in those days a well organised Commissariat, *was largely fed on frogs*. Eventually to distinguish themselves from other sections *they took the frog as their emblem and embroidered it on their banners*. As is shown by the old tapestries on the walls of Rheims Cathedral, as time went on the shape of the frog became more and more idealised, first the body became longer, then the shoulders were made broader, the hind legs shorter, and in the end the frog took on the appearance of a *Fleur de Lys* and has remained so ever since.

In the case of England, the emblem of the early Saxons was first a "bull" most probably due to the "lost ten Tribes" who came North with the Phœnicians and other races and settled in England. I have related earlier in these pages that Hebrew history tells us that the Ensign of the House of Joseph was an "engl" also written "angl," a bull, which in the end gave the name Engl-land to the country. Hundreds of years later the Romans took back with them captives from what they called Angleland and called them "Angles" which it is quite probable is the origin for Latin countries calling England, Angleterre, as they do to the present day.

As I explained earlier we have here then the origin of the symbolic figure for England being represented by "John Bull."

When the Normans conquered England in 1066 the Flag and crest of William the Conqueror was a single Lion rampant, but two generations later when his descendants laid claim to the three countries of England, Normandy and Brittany, they put three Lions on their banners, and so this emblem of the Lion has supplanted that of the Bull and has become the principal heraldic sign of Great Britain.

England's other national emblem the Unicorn, as I mentioned on page 65, is derived from a totally different source.

It is a curious fact that the only two great nations who have the emblem of the Lion in connection with their National Arms are Britain and Japan, and there is a mass of evidence which goes to prove that far off Japan was peopled by a part of Israel after they were driven from Samaria. This may account for the origin of the famous class called Samurai who proudly boast that they are the oldest race in Japan. It is also a curious fact that we find King Solomon was crowned in the Palace of Gihon and there exists in Japan also an ancient Palace called by exactly the same name—Gihon.

When one considers the symbolism contained in the Emblems and Ensigns of Nations, one is constrained to believe that some occult force or Divine inspiration, lies behind the meaning that one finds expressed in them. In the earliest days of the Israelites their Emblems or Standards were of an astrological foundation; history tells us that they marched out of bondage in Egypt under Standards representing the four divisions of the Zodiac. In Numbers, chapter ii, verse 2, we read "Every man of the children of Israel shall pitch *by his own standard, with the ensign of their father's house,*" and in Jeremiah the command is clearly given "Declare ye among the nations and publish and *set up a standard.*"

We will now consider the Standard and Heraldic emblems "set up and published" by the United States on their becoming a nation. History does not tell us who the men were, who obeying the orders of Congress worked out the Heraldic signs, emblems, and Seal of the United States.

If it is true that "by their fruits ye shall know them," then in this case we have every right to believe that such men, whoever they may have been, were not only inspired but were as well keen students of Astrology, for there are no "ensigns" or *emblems of any nation more pregnant with mysterious occult meaning and truth* than are those of the United States. In the first place these men evidently were well aware that their country was governed by the Sign of Gemini, and was *born as a Nation in that Sign.* Turning up the old work on Astrology I mentioned before, it distinctly states that "the colours of the Sign of Gemini are red blended with white" and so the Flag of the new Nation was ordered to be made with alternating stripes of *red and white.* Further, as Gemini is the first House in the Triplicity of Air, the Eagle, the King of the Air, was chosen as a special symbol—and perhaps one prophetic *that the United States is predestined to have dominion of the Air.* Glancing back to the copies of those old tablets on Astrology made in the times of the greatest astrologers the world has ever seen, I read "this sign (Gemini) governs all things relating to the air—machines that float on air and inventions relating to it of every kind." Strange, is it not, to look back and remember that it was owing to the work of two Americans, the brothers Orville and Wilbur Wright of Ohio, that flying machines and aeroplanes *were first brought into practical use.*[1]

[1]Colonel Linbergh's wonderful flight alone in the "Spirit of St. Louis" across the Atlantic to Paris, in June 1927, will also be remembered.—[Ed.]

The "spread eagle" is therefore in every sense a true symbol of the United States and may well be a promise of their future in the dominion of the Air.

History teaches us that the Eagle was one of the four standards under which the Israelites marched out of bondage to the Egyptians and further—while the other standards took up the positions assigned to them in the East, West, and South—the standard of the Eagle *was on the North*. It was thus indeed fitting in every way that Americans marching out from their bondage to the English, should have chosen the Eagle as their symbol—the Standard of the North of the ancient Israelites—the emblem of freedom and as I stated before the promise of their future conquest of the Air.

Let us now analyse a little more closely the symbol of the Eagle as engraved on the National Arms of the United States. In the right claw is an Olive branch—emblem of peace and plenty. In the left a bunch of pointed arrows—emblem of defence. Could any device be more appropriate? Could any have been better thought out? There is, however, still more to follow. When the United States became a Nation, she was composed of *thirteen* States, *thirteen* representatives signed the Declaration of Independence, *thirteen* stripes of alternating red and white floated on the first American flag together with its *thirteen* stars that Washington floated over his Camp and a salute of *thirteen* guns announced that fact to the world.

Turn back again to the American Eagle, you will find that the olive branch has *thirteen* leaves, also that there are *thirteen* arrows, and above the head of the Eagle are *thirteen* stars and in each wing there are *thirteen* feathers. Upon the scroll carried by the Eagle is the famous motto *E Pluribus Unum,* making *thirteen* letters.

On one side of the Great Seal of the United States of America is one of the most remarkable examples of symbolism that can be found among the Heraldic signs of any nation. It is an unfinished Pyramid built with *thirteen* steps rising from the base of solid rock, above suspended in the air is the Capstone with an "*all seeing eye*"; in the centre of the triangle and above it are the mystic words, "*Annuit Coeptis,*" again containing *thirteen* letters and meaning "He hath prospered our beginning," for the design is clearly intended to show, by the Capstone not having descended into its place, that the work is still unfinished. Underneath all is the explanatory motto full of meaning and deep significance—*Novus Ordo Seclorum* (a mighty order of Ages is born anew).

The Mace in the House of Representatives is made of *thirteen* ebony rods bound together by bands of silver. There are *thirteen* bars on the National Shield across the breast of the Eagle. These thirteen bars are joined to one Bar across the top which has in itself a peculiar occult meaning which I will now explain.

At first sight it would appear to those who do not understand the real significance of Numbers that *thirteen* is the representative number of the United States. From one point of view this is so, but it by no means covers the depth of meaning that is concealed by the number thirteen.

It must be borne in mind that as there are only nine planets controlling this Earth, so beyond the number Nine we cannot go as far as ordinary numbers are concerned. The numbers 1, 2, 3, 4, 5, 6, 7, 8, and 9, are what may be well called "mass chords of harmony" or "mass vibration." Ten is simply a repetition of 1 with a zero, an 11 can be reduced by addition, to the "mass chord" of 2, the 12 to a 3, the 13 to a 4, and so on with every number and no matter how many numbers a figure may make, all can be reduced by addition to a single digit which in its turn becomes *the root of the larger number and its basic principle.*

The "mass chord" therefore of the number thirteen which is so much in evidence in connection with the national affairs of the United States is 1 plus 3, a 4, for its single or "mass" number. This number in occultism, and in Astrology, stands for the planet Uranus. Both this planet, as well as its number, represents "a new order of things" and so bears out the motto engraved on the Great Seal of the United States, Novus Ordo Seclorum (a mighty order of Ages is born anew). In occultism this number of 4 is written as 4 hyphen 1, or simply 4-1 and stands for Uranus 4 and Sun 1. These numbers are called sympathetic or interchangeable with the number 2-7, which stand for the Moon 2 and Neptune 7, and are especially important if a person, a Nation or thing should be born or created on one of these numbers between the 21st June and the 21st July (period or House of the Moon and Neptune), or from the 22nd July to the 22nd August (period or House of the Sun and Uranus). It therefore follows that the most important numbers and dates which play the greatest rôle in the history of the United States are first, the series of the 4 and 1 such as the 1st, 4th, 10th, 13th, 19th, 22nd, 28th and 31st, and in a lesser or more minor way, the series of the 2 and 7, such as the 2nd, 7th, 11th, 16th 20th, 25th, and 29th, but on account of the importance of the Planet Uranus in the affairs of the United States 4 is *the basic or principal number.* This strange law of numbers will be found borne out in the most striking way as the following illustration shows, of "the mass chord" the 4-1 of the number thirteen in connection with

the symbolism of the United States, and dates of events influencing the affairs of the Nation.

Washington's Birthday (first President U.S.A.)	22 Feb.	representing	a	4
Declaration of Independence	4 July	,,	,,	4
George III (the King who brought about the war born	4 June	,,	,,	4
Continental Congress, Philadelphia	10 May	,,	,,	1
First Order for Troops in the Civil War	13 April	,,	,,	4
Surrender of Fort Sumter	13 April			4
Battle of Fort Donaldson	13 Feb.			4
Battle of Fredericksburg	13 Dec.			4
Admiral Dewey entered Manila Bay	1 May			1
Capture of Manila ..	13 Aug.			4
President Woodrow Wilson, born	28 Dec.	,,	,,	1
President Wilson arrived in France	13 Dec.	,,	,,	4
First convoy of Ships to Great War sailed ..	13 June	,,	,,	4
General Pershing born ..	13 Sept.	,,	,,	4
Decisive battle U.S. troops at St. Mihiel	13 Sept.	,,	,,	4
Joseph Jefferson (author of the Declaration of Independence) born ..	2 April	,,	,,	2
died	4 July	,,	,,	4
President McKinley, born	29 Jan.	,,	,,	2
Declared War with Spain	20 April	,,	,,	2
President James Munroe (famous for the Munroe doctrine) born	28 April	,,	,,	1
died	4 July	,,	,,	4

With an American History before them, my readers will have no difficulty in adding many other illustrations. I will now endeavour to explain a still more curious side of numbers which will explain more fully the significance of the number thirteen.

In my *Book of Numbers*,[1] recently published in England and America, I have given in detail the occult meaning of all the Numbers from 1 to 9, together with the meaning of what is called the "compound numbers," namely, all those after the "mass chords" 1, 2, 3, 4, 5, 6, 7, 8, 9. In this book I have explained that the numbers 1 to 9 "belong to the physical or material side of things and the 'compound numbers' from 10 on belong *to the more occult or spiritual side of life*." In other words, the "compound numbers" represent the *hidden forces* playing their part in the background of the person, nation, or thing, represented by the "compound number." The system I have given to the world is distinct and different from all other books that have been written on the occult side of Numbers. It is one I have proved myself after long years of professional work and personal study. It is the simplest one to use, the least confusing in method, and the most reliable of all the many systems I have examined. It is one that has been employed by the Masters of Occultism since the

[1] "Cheiro's" *Book of Numbers*. Herbert Jenkins Ltd.

most far distant ages. It has been kept concealed from the masses by secret occult societies and other means but is now released to the world at large on account of the "new age" we are so rapidly approaching.

The symbolism given to Numbers was originally set out in pictures and is so ancient that no one can tell from whence it came. I have endeavoured in my *Book of Numbers*, to which I have alluded, to translate this symbolism in clear language that any person of average intellect would be able to understand. For the purposes of the book before us I think it is only necessary to give the hidden or occult meaning to the number thirteen, which is the one that concerns the subject—the United States of which I am writing. But if readers wish to find out their own "fadic" or important number, it will be easy for them to get the book I have mentioned without confusing the issue which we are considering in these pages.

What I have written and published in my *Book of Numbers* on the meaning of the "compound" number thirteen is as follows:

"This is a Number indicating continual change of plans, place, and such like, and is *not* unfortunate as is generally supposed. In some ancient writings it is said 'He *who understands* the Number 13 *will be given power and dominion.*' . . . It is symbolised by the picture of a Skeleton, or Death with a scythe reaping down men. It is a Number of upheaval, destruction and re-creation. It is a symbol of Power which, *if wrongly used, will wreak destruction upon itself*. It is a number of warning if it becomes a 'compound' number in one's calculations." Looking back over the symbolic pictures in the old book from which I have translated the above passage, I find it further states "The Number 13 represents a New Age or a new order of things." This is completely in accordance with the idea expressed in the motto on the Great Seal of the United States "Novus Ordo Seclorum" and confirms what I said before that the men who were entrusted to create the Heraldic emblems of their Country, had a deep knowledge of Occultism and Astrology, and were doubtless inspired in doing this work.

That people are "inspired" in the work they are called on to do, is, even in this materialistic age, more or less acknowledged, therefore it may not be out of place to conclude this chapter on the selection of the emblems of the United States by the words of Isaiah, chapter 42, verse 16, "I will bring the blind by a way that they knew not; I will lead them in paths that they have not known; I will make darkness light before them, and crooked things straight."

Chapter VI

THE ORIGIN OF THE UNITED STATES AND ITS FUTURE ADVANCEMENT—(*Cont.*)

BEFORE we leave this question of the symbolism of the Eagle in connection with the Destiny of the United States, I would like to call attention to a most remarkable fact, or coincidence, call it what you will, in which the mysterious symbolism of the Eagle figured, towards the end of the Great War. Owing to the turmoil of the period and the subsequent conclusion of the terrible conflict the significance of the occurrence I am about to relate has been overlooked.

It is as follows: A new Star and one of *the first magnitude* suddenly appeared in the Constellation of Aquilat (the Eagle) on the night of Saturday, 8th June, 1918, about the time when the American Troops commenced their entry into the War. For fear people might think I am laying too much emphasis on such a fact as the appearance of this new Star, I will copy what appeared in the usually "matter of fact" *Times* of London under date of Thursday, 12th June, 1918:

"The appearance of a new star in the constellation Aquila, to which the Astronomer Royal (Sir Frank Dyson) drew attention in *The Times* of Monday has excited a great deal of interest. The present is certainly the most brilliant temporary star that has shone in the firmament since the celebrated one in 1604. *The new star will assuredly form one of the chief astronomical events of our time.*" In the same issue of this paper appeared another article headed "The New Star."

"A great white star has swam into our ken and it comes at a moment when humanity is looking for a new world. Certainly a new star of the first magnitude, discovered by several eyes at once and promptly vouched for by Greenwich, *is a portent.* Can we say more? May we hail it as an omen of victory in the great struggle between Might and Right? Would that we could. When in 1572 Tycho Brahe observed a new and brilliant star which shone like Jupiter that star ushered in the most brilliant period of English History, and perhaps this new star which is believed to be 'perfectly stellar' is an event on the threshold of our new age. Surely here, for the mystic mind, is an intimation of hope, not to this monarch or that, nor even to that nation or this, but to mankind at large, even as the Star of Bethlehem was an intimation that a new era was opening for the wearied sons of men. The star comes at a moment not altogether incomparable with that moment of the birth of Christ when the Roman world was sated. It has come when the world is again at a turning point."

Such was the account in *The Times* of the appearance of "one of the chief astronomical events of our time," but many of the indications of still deeper significance have been overlooked, as for example the Star suddenly shone out of the heavens on Saturday night, June 8th, 1918, on the completion of six months to even a day from December 9th, 1917, the day when the Turks surrendered Jerusalem, and exactly three months before the American Troops under General Pershing won a decisive battle of the War by the breaking through of the salient of St. Mihiel on September 13th. Another point to which not enough attention has been given, is that this star appeared in the constellation of Aquila, the Eagle, the symbol in Heraldry of the United States, and just five months and a few days before the Armistice was signed on the 11th November. This star appeared in one of the most critical periods of the Great War *in the constellation of the Eagle*, and it is admitted by all unprejudiced observers that it was due to the fact that because the United

States poured her fresh troops into the War zone that the morale of the German Army and the German Nation behind it acknowledged themselves beaten.

It has also been overlooked that as this star rose in the East the Sun at the other side of the world was in eclipse, *which was the only total eclipse of the Sun during the year* 1918. To those who are privileged to have "a mystic mind" it would appear that in the inscrutable wisdom of the Lord of Hosts or Lord of the Heavens a significant message was sent to all mankind foreshadowing the very cause of the end of the War, and at the same time calling attention to the beginning of the fulfilment of "the promise" to the chosen of Israel, that "the Times of the Gentiles" were coming to an end, that Jerusalem was freed from the thraldom of centuries and the Land promised to them as their inheritance was about to be restored.

Another very remarkable occurrence took place when this new star appeared in the constellation of the Eagle on Saturday, the 8th June, 1918. *On that very day* one of the largest ships in the British Navy was launched and the name given to this ship was *H.M.S. Eagle.* This coincidence, if we must call it by such a word, was emphasised by the fact that it came into the minds of His Majesty King George's Ministers that the King's express approval might be given for the *wife of the American Ambassador* to be present at this launch and *for her to give the name of the Eagle to the ship.* The following is the notice of this event that appeared in the pages of *The Times* on Thursday, 13th June, 1918.

"The United States Naval Headquarters in London announce that Mrs. Page, wife of the American Ambassador, named H.M.S. Eagle, one of the largest ships in the British Navy at her launch at Messrs. Armstrong Whitworth & Co.'s yard on the Tyne on Saturday. Mrs. Page was invited to be the official sponsor for the Eagle by Sir Eric Geddes, the first Lord of the Admiralty, with the express approval of the King."

And this is still not all in this strange story of coincidences (?). Although this ship is described in *The Times* account as "one of the largest ships in the British Navy," she was not a battleship as might be inferred but an *Aircraft carrier, the largest of her kind* and one that cost the huge sum of Four Million Pounds.

CHAPTER VII

THE DESTINY OF THE UNITED STATES

AS I have explained in a former chapter, the numbers 4-1 and the planets Uranus and the Sun have great importance in connection with the Destiny of the United States with its Zodiacal ruler the Sign of Gemini, the positive House of the planet Mercury.

The Sun, emblem of wealth, together with Mercury, emblem of commerce, business, speculation and invention, are the distinctive planets of this Nation, this combination with Uranus the planet of "the new age" and "new thought" was a promise from the very commencement of unprecedented prosperity for the United States.

The influence of the basic number 4, the number of Uranus, caused this nation to plan out for itself *a new idea of Government* and the election of Congress *every four years* instead of following the English idea of a government elected every seven years. As the planet Uranus is the special planet of Democracy and represents "the people," the real Government of the United States will always remain in the hands of "the people" and the Autocracy of any one "leader" will never last long in such a nation. The control of the masses will always be the "crux" of the situation in such a country, and in the coming years will present ever increasing difficulties. From 1929 the Government will have to be prepared to meet a new programme containing some startling proposals which will be put forward by Labour Leaders, together with a rapid increase of Communistic and Bolshevick ideas and the employment of "the bomb" and dynamite to enforce their demands.[1]

During 1929 and the following years and until the God of War again unsheathes the sword, lawlessness and crime will be on the increase and will sweep the country from end to end. The Government will be severely criticised for both its home and foreign policy and in the next few years many of the States will commence a movement which will become more and more active—for the *individual control of their own affairs*—especially on the subject of prohibition and the Divorce Laws. The immediate result of this will be, that some States will be prohibition States,

[1]The execution of Sacco and Vanzetti and the "bomb" outrages during 1927 will be remembered.—[Ed.]

and others the reverse in accordance with the individual vote of each community.[1]

The Foreign policy of the Government during the next few years will be taken to task on account of the attitude of the United States towards some Foreign Power which will be distasteful to the general public.[2]

For the coming five years an enormous expansion of trade will take place in such Industries as Steel and Iron, Machinery of all kinds and armament works, especially with such countries as China, South Africa, South America, Russia, Turkey and Palestine, and increasingly large fortunes will be made in such lines of business during these years.

The "Oil Interests" of the United States will become involved in a keen struggle with British interests in various parts of the world.[3]

The Customs situation in Mexico will loom up with increasing importance and developments will arise that will call for the exercise of great patience and diplomacy. War in this quarter may be put off for some time, but not for long. The eventual destiny of the United States will force her to become the guardian both of Mexico and all other countries as far south as the Panama Canal.

[1] The State of Nevada commenced this action in the Spring of 1931.

[2] The Naval Agreement with England during 1930.

[3] The English Shell Oil Co. under-bid U.S.A. Oil Companies in the early months of 1931 for the supply of Crude Petroleum and Petrol for the Japanese Navy.

During 1927 a powerful American financial combination will be formed for the purchase or control of Rubber Plantations in various parts of the world, and an intense commercial struggle will commence between American and British interests for the control of this commodity. The export of "carbon black" as an ingredient in the manufacture of rubber tyres and for printing ink will so increase in price that England and European Countries will be forced to restrict the size of newspapers and the output of rubber tyres. This will give the United States industries an enormous advantage until England, Germany and France discover a new commodity to take the place of "carbon black," which undoubtedly will come about.[1]

I wrote these predictions in 1925, that the United States would buy up enormous Rubber Plantations in the next few years, which is attested to by the Editor at the commencement of this book.

These predictions are now confirmed by the announcement published lately in American and English newspapers on the 15th September, 1927. The following extract is taken from *The Evening News* of London of that date, headed:

[1]The U.S.A. is the principal producer of "carbon black" in the world, and the export price has recently increased by nearly one hundred per cent.

"U.S. Dream of a Rubber Empire"

"Into the World Rubber War to-day enters Mr. Henry Ford—reputed to be the world's richest man, and certainly so rich that he can have no idea of what he is worth.

His first move is a characteristic Ford move—a move made to the tune of £8,000,000, as this cable shows:

New York. Thursday.

'According to the *New York World* to-day Mr. Henry Ford has bought 1,200,000 acres of land in Para, Brazil, for £8,000,000, and is trying to obtain an additional 2,800,000 acres.

'All the land will be used for rubber plantations.'—Reuter.

Heads of many American motor and tyre concerns have for long been involved in the Rubber War. But between them and Mr. Ford there is great difference—they have their fellow-directors and shareholders to consider and consult. Mr. Ford has nobody but himself to consider. The Ford concern has no shareholders outside the Ford family.

A 'War' of Millions

It is significant that Mr. Henry Ford was one of the most important witnesses before the House of Representatives Committee which sat at Washington a few years ago to investigate rubber prices, and it is well known that he is a staunch supporter of Mr. Hoover, who when he was U.S. Secretary of Commerce, denounced the British Restriction Scheme.

In rubber circles it has been known for some time that America has been preparing plans to make serious inroads on Britain's rubber monopoly, and this latest move by Mr. Ford is likely to have widespread developments.

In every effort which has been made in recent years influential support has been given by Mr. Hoover, who has openly said that the British Scheme 'must be defeated.'

America uses about 70 per cent. of the world's rubber supply, when the Department of Commerce recently published the results of its investigation on increased prices, American newspapers, taking their cue from Mr. Harvey Firestone, head of the Firestone tyre manufacturing firm, indulged in crude calculations designed to show that the difference between the old and the new price of rubber coincided approximately with the annual payments on the British debt.

The American Rubber Association made a big move in recent years, when, with the help of Mr. Hoover, they opened negotiations with Holland for the establishment of American plantations in Dutch possessions.

Two new projects were launched recently in New York, one being a plan by the Rubber Association to spend £2,000,000 annually for five years in creating or buying plantations in the Philippines and Sumatra and for stimulating the greater production of wild rubber, particularly in Brazil.

The second was Mr. Hoover's plan to form a corporation of which all the subscribers would be motor-car manufacturers, to acquire plantations in the far corners of the world.

Mr. Firestone formulated a scheme, involving £20,000,000 of capital, for the establishment of a U. S. rubber empire in Liberia—and so the battle has gone on.

Mr. Hoover has alleged that in 1925 Britain was extorting £140,000,000 a year from the American public by her Rubber restrictions.

Some astounding inventions in relation to aerial navigation will, in the next few years, be made in the United States. A process for the cheap production of a non-inflammable gas like Helium will be discovered and will cause a greater development in the use of Airships than has ever been dreamed of before.[1] The United States will grasp this opportunity to bring about the complete conquest of the Air which, as I explained in a previous chapter, is foreshadowed by the Eagle being the National emblem and the country, as a whole, being under the Sign of Gemini—the First Triplicity of Air. The nations that will run her very close for this supremacy will be England and Germany, but the Zodiacal Sign of these countries being Aries in the House of Mars, their development will be along the lines of Engines of Destruction which will have no equal in the next war.

To England will remain the "kingdom of the sea," as a "carrier" for the produce of other nations she will steadily increase the supremacy she at present holds.

During the coming years enormous loans of money will be floated in America for foreign countries and large shipments of rails, motors and machinery of all kinds will be the result. American capital will exploit an immense deposit of coal which will be found in the Central States, large enough to supply the world with fuel, but at the same time a new method of extraction of oil from coal will be perfected at such a low cost that all machinery together with ships and trains

[1]The Oil Wells of the U.S.A. produce more Helium gas than all the other Petroleum fields in the world put together.

will be driven by a new power derived from it and steam engines will become things of the past.

American interests in China will before long cause a rupture with Japan which will threaten war between the two countries.

When this friction with Japan crops up, Mexico will take advantage of the situation to force a readjustment of the "silver question" which at the present moment is crippling her advancement, and preventing the developement of her industries.

In the coming years some form of "guerilla-war" will break out in Mexico which will involve the United States. This will give Japan the opportunity of fighting for the supremacy of the Pacific Ocean, her first move will be to take possession of the Philipine Islands, cutting off America's coal base and Naval station. This war will last for many years and will not be decided by "force of arms." Japan will be given undisputed possession of the richest parts of the Far East. In the end all the Foreign Powers will be cleared out of the East, and China and Japan as United nations will control that part of the globe.

After the Armageddon which I will describe in a following chapter, the "zone of influence" of the United States will extend from the Arctic Ocean to the Panama Canal. She will become the great Trading Centre of the East and West, and her supremacy in the Western Hemisphere will endure for a period of about seven hundred years from the date of her Declaration of Independence in 1776.

The "fadic" or important dates in the history of the United States appear to coincide so mysteriously with those concerning the past history of the Israelites and the promise of their return to their own land that it forces one to come to the conclusion that the United States will in the near future play a most important rôle in the opening up and development of Palestine. "The Precession of the Equinoxes" which I have alluded to before, giving periods of time that average 2150 years, fits in with the destiny of the United States as they have done with the history of the Israelites. This mysterious period of years is considered by many students of such things to foreshadow the length of time known as "The Times of the Gentiles" when Jerusalem would be "trodden under foot," and the many prophecies that when this time would be fulfilled the Israelites would return to power must, to my mind, be fulfilled just as other prophecies concerning this race have been fulfilled in the past. The difficulty being solely to establish when "the Times of the Gentiles" commenced, for if this could be once and for all definitely settled the rest would be only a matter of simple calculation.

Taking all the circumstances under consideration, it seems only reasonable to assume that this commencement date should be taken as the year when the Assyrians under Nebuchadnezzar overcame Jerusalem. This date is generally taken to be about 770 B.C. and as 700 to 720 years appears to be a cycle of special importance to the Israelites, three of these cycles from 770 B.C. would bring us to A.D. 1490, which is on or about the date of the discovery of the American Continent and a date in the world's history when the Jews were beginning to come back into power. Another of these cycles of 700 to 720 years will bring us approximately to the close of one of "the precession" periods when the Israelites will not only fulfil the promise of inheriting "the land of their forefathers," but the United States will also commence to fill its greater destiny and one, I predict, in close connection with the opening up of Palestine and the surrounding countries.

Chapter VIII

THE MYSTERY OF THE TWELVE TRIBES OF ISRAEL

THE RETURN TO THE "HOUSE OF JUDAH AND ISRAEL" TO "THE LAND GIVEN TO THEIR FOREFATHERS"

THAT the Israelites were a "chosen race" for exhibiting the Design and plan of the Creator will, I think, be evident to anyone who will take the trouble to examine the history of this people with an unprejudiced and impartial mind.

Why this should have been so, is but one of the many mysteries of Design that may be clearly seen in the evolution of that Divine plan which appears to have *the development of mankind* as its *central purpose.*

As in the Solar System a planet such as the Earth appears to have been selected for a special purpose, there is no reason why a race should not have also been selected to carry out and make manifest "the inscrutable purpose of God." In Deuteronomy, chapter vii, verses 6, 7 and 8, are the following startling words:

"The Lord thy God *hath chosen thee* to be a special people unto Himself, above all people that are upon the face of the earth. The Lord did not set his love upon you, nor choose you, because ye were more in number than any people; for ye were the fewest of all people: but because the Lord loved you, and because he would keep the oath which he had sworn unto your fathers."

Apart from records given us in the Bible, we know from histories of other races that the Israelites did exist, that Abraham lived in Ur of the Chaldees, that they were for over four hundred years in bondage to the Egyptians and that they finally possessed for a time the land of Palestine, built a City called Jerusalem, and had Kings whose names and deeds are recorded on the monuments of other races who also existed in those far off days.

Apart from the symbolism and allegorical description that has been associated with the Israelites and the part they have played in the history of the world, there remains the most overwhelming proof that the great episodes that marked the march of this race through the ages down to the present time, actually took place. We know from Egyptian history that such a man as Joseph became a ruler and a Prince in Egypt, that the Exodus under Moses took place, that Solomon built the first

Temple in Jerusalem and that the Queen of Sheba and other potentates testified to his greatness.

All the other principal events in the history of this race are also corroborated, the Babylonian Captivity, the building of the second Temple, the existence of the third in the days of Herod and the ultimate destruction of Jerusalem when, as predicted, "one stone was not left upon another" are equally authenticated.

But behind this record is another, that stands out clear and distinct on the pages of Time, the most wonderful mystery of all, namely, that the events thus recorded were *the fulfilment of prophecies equally recorded generations before such events took place.*

There is no other race in the world of which the same can be said. What then, we may well ask, is the mystery and the message of it all?

No reasonable being to-day denies that behind the Creation of the world there is a "First Cause," a Creator who brought the world into existence, and further, so designed it and its Solar System, that from its greatest marvel down to its smallest atom, they one and all exhibit *design, plan, and above all, purpose,* which *cannot be set aside or disputed.*

It is in such considerations that the prophecies related in that great record of history, the Bible, have their importance. It is simply a logical proposition that the Designer, in setting certain laws into action, knew the after effect of such laws and therefore prophecies that such and such an event would take place could be made by those who were inspired to fortell such things, generations and centuries in advance.

Such prophecies were veiled under the language of allegory—some hidden beneath the exotic flowers and imagery of Oriental expression, while some again were deliberately concealed from the common people by priests of different religions, who lived at the same period as the Israelites.

We are distinctly informed that years before the event, God gave Moses directions for the Temple his descendant would build and of which "he showed him the pattern in the heavens," and years later when the Temple came to be erected, we find that Solomon carried out "the pattern in the heavens" in such detail that it had twelve divisions to represent the twelve constellations of the heavens and the twelve tribes of Israel, together with an "inner court" of again twelve divisions. The jewels on the breastplate of the High Priest, emblematic of the hidden meaning of the twelve signs of the Zodiac, were very distinctly commanded "And the stones shall be with the names of the children of Israel, twelve, according to their names . . .

every one with his name shall they be according to the twelve tribes." (Ex. xxviii, 21.)

Josephus says "Whether any one wish to refer the twelve stones to the twelve months, or to the same number of constellations in the Zodiac, he will not wander far from *the real meaning*."

History tells us that the Tribes of Israel marched out of Egypt in four divisions corresponding to the four cardinal points of the heavens, each division under a standard representing their position in the Zodiac. Further back still we have the record of Jacob giving names to the twelve Tribes in exact accordance with the meaning attached even to-day to the signs of the Zodiac—that wonderful pathway in the heavens which is one of the greatest mysteries of creation.

That the Israelites were for some unaccountable reason a race set apart for the manifestation of the God Power in connection with the Destiny of mankind, is I think, evident from the prophecies concerning them. That they were also intended to be an example of the mysterious influence of the planets on human life appears to be equally evident.[1]

The Twelve Tribes as symbols of the twelve divisions of the Zodiac are not mere coincidences and neither is the mystic influence of

[1] "Out of Heaven (or the Heavens) He made thee to hear His voice; that *He might instruct thee*." (Deut. iv, 36.)

numbers in connection with their history. All through the story of the Israelites, in fact all through the Bible, the power of the Seven Creative planets is not only distinctly emphasised, but in all cases represents the mysterious "God Force" in nature. A few examples of this will make this idea more clear.

For seven days God commanded the Israelites to march round Jericho, seven priests to bear seven trumpets, and at the sound of the trumpets on the seventh day, the walls of Jericho fell—before the mysterious Law of Vibration or "God Force" symbolised by the number seven.

In the fifth chapter of Revelations, we read, "The seven Spirits of God sent forth into all the earth"; also in the first chapter, "The seven stars are the angels of the seven churches" (or planets), and in the fourth chapter, "Seven lamps of fire burning before the throne which are the seven Spirits of God."

We may also note that the Temple of Solomon which was built according to the "pattern of the heavens" had to take seven years in its erection, and also that there were exactly seven generations between David and the destruction of Jerusalem by the Romans.

That the Israelites had a knowledge of two other planets beyond the Seven so often alluded to, is in evidence in their Book of

Zohar, together with the fact that the entire nine planets to whom numbers were given were the basis of all material calculation on this earth, for beyond the figures 1, 2, 3, 4, 5, 6, 7, 8 and 9, we cannot go, the 10 being simply a repetition of the first number 1 with a zero added, as I have explained earlier in these pages. The number 9 thus became the number representing *materiality or man*: this is borne out by that strange verse in the thirteenth chapter of Revelations, where it states "*the number of man is* 666." These cryptic numbers added together produce 18 which is 1 plus 8—a 9, *or the number of materiality or of man.*

It is a curious fact that the number concealed in the name Adam is twelve times twelve, or 144, which is the mystic number of the Zodiac with its twelve divisions and which number again conceals the number 9 as may be seen by the addition of 144 together, producing as it does the number of the planets of our Solar System—and, as we have seen previously, *the number of Man.*

That this ancient people were well versed in the mysterious influence of the Zodiac and the action of the planets since the time of Seth, the third son of Adam, is borne out by history. We have, as well, the statement of Josephus to the effect that Abraham taught the Egyptians the knowledge of Astrology, and even Solomon wrote that his great wisdom was derived from the study of such things.

"For He hath given me certain knowledge of the things that are, to know how the world was made, and the operation of the elements. The beginning, ending and midst of times, *the alterations of the turning of the Sun*, and the change of seasons. The circuits of years, and the position of stars. The nature of living creatures and the thoughts of men.

"All things that are either secret or manifest I learned. For He who is the Creator of all things taught me."[1]

That the power of Israel would be broken, her cities destroyed and her people dispersed to the four corners of the earth was foreshadowed by prophecies made generations before such events took place. It will be sufficient to quote only one or two of such prophecies here.

"But if thou wilt not hearken to the voice of the Lord thy God to do and observe all His commandments, the Lord shall bring thee unto a nation which neither thou nor thy fathers have known; and thou shalt become an astonishment, a proverb, and a byword among all nations whither the Lord shall lead thee." (Deut. xxviii, verses 36 and 37.)

[1] The Apocrypha, or the Wisdom of Solomon. Chap. VII. 17 to 22.

"The Lord shall bring a nation against thee . . . a nation whose tongue thou shalt not understand. A nation of fierce countenance which shall not regard the person of the old, nor show favour to the young." (Deut. xxviii, 49.)

I need hardly call attention to the fact that every word in these prophecies have been fulfilled.

Strangely enough, as if some great law of nature was employed as the instrument for the breaking of this powerful combination of tribes, we find that as long as they remained of the number of Twelve in accordance with the signs of the Zodiac, their progress was that of continual increase of power. A time however came when ten tribes split away from the Twelve and endeavoured to become a nation to themselves. From the moment of this division the magic circle of Twelve was broken: the harmonious influence of the magnetic Zodiac was destroyed, and in the decline of the power of Israel a great lesson was taught to all other nations.

The break in the magic circle of the Twelve had nearly occurred once before but then *it was immediately repaired.* I allude to the time when the Tribe of Benjamin, as related in the Book of Judges, chapter 21, fought against the other Tribes and was almost annihilated. In the fifteenth verse, we read:

"And the people repented them for Benjamin, because that the Lord had *made a breach in the tribes of Israel.*"

The elders of the remaining Tribes took counsel and said "There must be an inheritance for them that be escaped of Benjamin, *that a tribe be not destroyed out of Israel.*"

This breach in the Twelve was at that time repaired and the nation of Israel went on in progress as before.

The final break did not take place until after the death of Solomon when jealousy against the Central Power of Jerusalem caused the ten tribes to revolt. This time the power of the Circle of Twelve was broken completely—the penalty was paid, and a little later the whole of what was known as the nation of Israel was made captive by the Assyrians, and a hundred years afterwards the remaining two tribes were conquered by the Babylonians and Jerusalem was destroyed.

These remaining tribes were in reality three, for during the reign of Rehoboam the tribe of Levi had returned to Jerusalem and was carried into captivity with Judah and Benjamin. On the return of these tribes they rebuilt Jerusalem and from *that time onward they were for the first time called Jews* and have been *known as Jews ever since.*

From the date of the Assyrian conquest,

"the ten tribes" became "lost" or "scattered among the heathen" as had been predicted in Lev. xxvi. That they continued to exist "among the heathen" is borne out by Josephus who writing in A.D. 70 said: "The entire body of the ten tribes are still beyond the river Euphrates, an immense multitude not to be estimated by numbers."

Those who have studied closely the History of the Jews believe that during the persecution and crucifixion of Christ, the Tribe of Benjamin, at that time in Jerusalem, took no part in it. At the destruction of Jerusalem by the Romans according to Josephus, this tribe escaped the massacre "as they had fled from the city and had joined the 'lost Tribes of Israel' beyond the Euphrates." This action of the Tribe of Benjamin had been actually foreshadowed some hundreds of years previously by the prophet Jeremiah in his predictions "O, ye children of Benjamin, gather yourselves to flee out of the midst of Jerusalem . . . for evil appeareth out of the north and great destruction." (Jer. vi, 1).

The siege and fall of Jerusalem in the reign of Titus A.D. 70, was accompanied by destruction and horrors worse than anything witnessed by the world either before or since. History tells us that over a million Jews were massacred at the capture of the City. The last stand against the triumphant Roman legions was in defence of the Temple; it is recorded that "the dead were heaped higher than the Altar," and that "human blood flowed down the Temple steps like a river." About seventy years later the Jews scattered through Palestine again revolted against the Roman rule. On this occasion no mercy whatever was shown to them; those who escaped death were sold into slavery or driven into far off countries, and the once fertile land of Palestine, its towns and villages, became a scene of the most absolute desolation, fulfilling the prophecies made generations before, that if the Twelve Tribes broke the covenant of the Lord they should be "dispersed," "their cities made desolate," and as the prophet Hosea wrote, "Israel shall be lost among the Gentiles" and "they shall be wanderers among the nations."

Although the ten tribes of Israel at the time of Christ had been "dispersed" after the Assyrian captivity for more than 700 years, they were even referred to by Christ on different occasions. "Go to the lost sheep of the house of Israel" was one of his commands to his disciples. Again he declared: "I am not sent but unto the lost sheep of the house of Israel." That the Jews in Palestine knew what he meant is shown by their words: "Will he go unto *the dispersed* among the Gentiles." (John vii, 35.)

The reason for the loss of power of the great Israelite nation commenced in the first instance with the break of the Twelve Tribes representative of the Twelve Houses of the Zodiac at the time of the fight with the Tribe of Benjamin at the battle of Gibeah, which I previously mentioned, and if one required greater proof of this, one will find it in the ninth verse of the tenth chapter of Hosea, in these striking words: "O Israel, thou hast sinned *from the days of Gibeah.*"

The second and complete break took place at the revolt of the ten tribes against Jerusalem. From this moment the harmony of the Twelve Tribes and the Twelve divisions of the Zodiac was ended. Keeping this idea in view, those mystic words that occur so often as to "the breaking of the covenant" between the Lord of Hosts and the Children of Israel, will be seen in a new light, and the story of Creation and the history of mankind will wear a broader view than is given to it by the narrow dogma of various religions which have appeared from time to time.

What became of the "lost Tribes" and what will be their ultimate destiny, I will endeavour to explain in subsequent chapters.

Chapter IX

THE FUTURE OF THE JEWS FORESHADOWED IN THE GREAT PYRAMID

THE ORIGIN OF THE GREAT PYRAMID AND ITS OCCULT MEANING

BEFORE we examine further the coming destiny of the Children of Israel, we must now consider the evidence which links this "peculiar people" with the greatest Monument and "Measurer of Time" that exists in the world, namely, the Great Pyramid.

The mystery of who built this colossal monument has never been solved. My own view is that it dates back to a period of time far beyond what has been generally ascribed to it; the line of reasoning I have taken is the following:

Noah had four sons and history tells us that one of their descendants, called Mizraim, Mizraim or Menes, became the first King of Egypt. Egyptian legends inform us that a King called Mizraim was famous as an

Astrologer. We know to-day that whoever built the Great Pyramid was a man who must have had an almost superhuman knowledge of the celestial bodies. It is reasonable then to assume that its architect and builder must have been this Mizraim, a descendant of Noah. Further, it would only be natural that such a man as one of the descendants of Noah who knew about the Deluge, would commemorate it by building a Monument as a record for future generations—and one *that no future flood could destroy.*

That there was some Divine plan or Design underlying such a marvellous creation must be apparent to any one who makes even a casual study of the subject, and that this plan or design is linked up with the Children of Israel and contains in its record exact periods of years corresponding to the great events in their history, stands out also in bold relief against the dark background of time.

That such a colossal monument, the wonder of all ages, one that has defied the ravages of Time, and exhibits in every detail the most minute mathematical accuracy in regard to astronomical laws, was only built as a Tomb for some King, is on the face of it absurd.

On the contrary, it is far more logical to assume that behind the words of Isaiah, chapter xix, verses 19 and 20, lies the true meaning of why such a monument was created: "In that day shall there be an altar to the Lord *in the midst of the land of Egypt*, and a pillar at the border thereof to the Lord. And it shall be *for a sign and for a witness* unto the Lord of Hosts *in the land of Egypt*."

I claim that the real meaning of the Great Pyramid is an astrological one setting forth the religion of Life, and God's purpose towards man as revealed by a study of the heavens, and that it will be through the sciences of Astrology and Astronomy that the mystery and reason for its construction will one day be made clear.

It has recently been demonstrated that the Great Pyramid contained exact measurements that denote to a fraction the number of days in a Solar year, and the mysterious period of time known as "the Precession of the Equinoxes."

It also contained the Hebrew sacred cubit which thousands of years later was employed by Solomon in the building of the first Temple and became the standard measurement for following civilisations, and from which the English inch owes its origin. Further, the mysterious empty sarcophagus found in recent times in the King's Chamber for some unexplained reason contains *the same capacity as did the Ark of the Covenant*.

Lastly, the length of the diagonals of its base when added together give to a fraction the number of years, 25,850 of the "Precession of the Equinoxes," that mysterious cycle of time so linked up with the destiny of the earth.

Such things could not come about by chance, but point to the fact that the Great Pyramid was definitely created to be *a measurer of time for some pre-determined purpose.*

Let us now see if from this we can get some information as to the Divine purpose and plan that lies behind this mysterious Monument "in the land of Egypt."

We have noticed earlier the argument that God for some reason created a certain race of people called Israelites to be "chosen" or "special people" to make manifest laws of nature and to fulfil prophecies made, in some cases, thousands of years before the events took place. In Deut. vii, 6, we read, "The Lord thy God hath chosen thee to be a special people unto Himself."

On the breaking of what is distinctly stated was "a Covenant," and which break was also clearly foreshadowed, this nation was dispersed to all parts of the earth, until such time when again, in fulfilment of prophecies, the children of Israel and Judah will possess the land of their forefathers. "Hear the word of the Lord, O ye nations, and declare it in the isles afar off and say, He that scattered

Israel will gather him, and keep him, as a shepherd doth his flock." (Jer., xxxi, 10.)

Again we read, "For lo, the days come, saith the Lord . . . and I will cause them to return to the land that I gave to their fathers, and they shall possess it." (Jer., xxx, 3.)

Looking back to the mystery of the Great Pyramid, we find with other measurements associated with it that it is also intended to be a great measurer of years. It is, in fact, the Solar-Lunar Clock of the Universe.

The Queen's Chamber which, in my judgment, represents the Moon, is placed directly under the apex of the Pyramid, while the King's Chamber, the most important of the two, has a distinct position of its own, and also by its larger size, represents the Sun.

Julius Cæsar, about 45 B.C., made the famous Julian Calendar by the aid of the most eminent mathematicians of those times. By A.D. 325 the Council of Nice discovered this calendar wrong by about ten days and it took civilisation until 1582 to discover the more accurate Gregorian Calendar, but owing to the difference of religion between Protestant and Catholic, it was not adopted in England and other Protestant countries until 1752.

Yet during all this long period Time was being measured without a flaw, by the Solar-Lunar Cycles exemplified in the Pyramid, which are the natural measures of Time given by the Creator of the Heavens from far distant ages.

It has lately been established that the periods of 1260 and 2300 years which are mentioned in the Book of Daniel and in the Apocalypse *are Solar-Lunar cycles;* and further, the difference between these two periods which is 1040 years, *is the largest accurate Solar-Lunar cycle known.*

For over nineteen centuries astronomers and chronologists have been trying to discover such a law of perfection in relation to time not knowing that for past ages it was clearly set out in the Book of Daniel, to anyone who would take the trouble to study its inspired prophecies.

The question is how did Daniel discover these marvellously accurate celestial cycles, at a time when probably there were no scientific instruments available—the answer must be the same as to who built the Pyramid with such a wealth of mathematical accuracy?

The same inspiration which gave the Architect of the Great Pyramid such a profound knowledge of calculation and the planets, undoubtedly inspired Daniel both in his prophecies and in his calculations of cycles of time, that contain in themselves perhaps the secrets of coming events.

As I said previously the mystery of the

Great Pyramid is the calculation of the exact length or duration of the "Precession of the Equinoxes," and the rate of the "precess" is the key to Astronomy and also to the great events in history both past, present and future.

The distinct "chiselled line" found in the descending passage of the Great Pyramid, denotes that at midnight in the Autumnal Equinox in the year 2150 B.C., the then Polar Star *à Draconis* shone down the descending passage to this "chiselled line" *the only mark of its kind in the Pyramid.*

I disagree with other writers who assert that this strangely recorded date must have been the date of the completion of the building of the Pyramid. I take this date to show a time in the history of the world of some extraordinary occurence and one so marked *that from it other dates might be calculated.*

Taking this date to commemorate such a great event as "the promise" given to Abraham, 2150 B.C. becomes a decided milestone in the history of the past when *the nation of Israel came into existence.*

From Abraham to the final fall and destruction of Jerusalem is a cycle of approximately 2150 years, and at its close, the Gentile Nations came into power. From this to the end of A.D. 2150 is another distinct span. At its close history in all probability will repeat itself—the law of the rise and fall of the wave of time will become manifest and the Israelites for the following period of 2150 years will be in the ascendant.

Let us now, using this distinct cycle of years which has provided us with a key to unlock other mysteries of time, sub-divide this great period to arrive at the dates of the more minor events in history.

Taking the same law of the Precession of the Equinoxes we find that the rate of the "precess" for *each degree* of the Zodiac is exactly seventy years and nine months.

We are told in the Scripture that the length of man's life is three score years and ten, or in other words, one degree of the movement of the Precession of the Equinoxes of *one day* measured by the Solar clock of the Universe.

If we now multiply this distinct period of seventy years by ten, we get another mysterious cycle of 700 years.

From the date of such an important occurrence as the destruction of Jerusalem, looking backwards, this cycle gives us the zenith of power of the Assyrian nation, the captivity of the ten tribes, and their complete loss of name as a nation.

Looking forward from the date of the destruction of Jerusalem, the cycle brings us to A.D. 700, the date of the commencement of Mohammedan power, and their conquest of

Egypt. Add to this again the 700 years cycle and we get 1400, the century in which the discovery of America was made, an epoch of enormous importance in the destiny of mankind.

Taking the discovery of America as a point of great meaning and adding the 700 cycle we reach the greater Primordial date of A.D., 2100 allowing for fractions in the precess of the equinox. This date should see *the new world of America approaching the commencement of a period of greatness and power*—the magnitude of which at this moment it is impossible to estimate.[1]

This important date for the Continent of America coincides with the same date given for the return of the Israelites into their own land, and the commencement of the Twelve Tribes as one nation, fulfilling the prophecy of Jeremiah, "In those days the House of Judah shall walk with the House of Israel and they shall come together out of the Land of the North to the land that I have given for an inheritance unto your Fathers." (Jer. iii, 18.)

History shows clearly that the Children of Israel as a race were for some mysterious reason dominated by the number seven.

Their record of the Creation of the world is given in a sevenfold period of time.

[1]This date 2100 closely fits in with the period given by the Precession of the Equinoxes 2150 years and also the commencement of the new Aquarian Age.

Their great teacher, Moses, laid down the rule that man's life was a span of seventy years, or ten times seven.

The Jubilee Cycle established as one of their institutions under the law of Moses was seven times seven or forty-nine years, and their greater Jubilee was to be seventy times seven.

Years before it took place the seventy years Captivity in Babylon was foretold to them.

The 490 years of their restoration to the final destruction of Jerusalem was an exact period predicted by Daniel of seven times seventy years.

From the birth of the Hebrew nation under Abraham to their entrance into the promised Land of Canaan, as closely as it is possible to calculate, was also 490 years, or seventy times seven.

From Joshua's conquest of Canaan to their first kingdom under Saul was 490 years.

From Saul their first king to their last and capture of Jerusalem by Nebuchadnezzar was 490 years, and from this event to the final destruction of Jerusalem by the Romans, was another period of 490 years.

After this calamity, which had been predicted long before the event, the strange cycle of seven commenced again.

In A.D. 70 Titus destroyed the Temple. Seventy years later came their second rebellion against the Romans and complete dispersion.

For a period of 490 years or again seventy times seven the Jews were lost in oblivion, from this and for another period of seventy times seven, or 490 years, was a cycle of the most intense persecution. At the end of this period the Mohammedan power began to wane (980) and the Jews once more began to make themselves felt in the world.

In the next period of seventy times seven, came the discovery of America and from this date to the next culminating point which will be reached in 1980, the Jews, or as they will again be called, Israelites, will have made enormous strides in wealth, world position and power.

From 1980 the succeeding period of another seventy times seven will, in my opinion, see the restoration of the Twelve Tribes of Israel as the dominant power in the World.

During this period it will be the Israelites and nations who have intermingled with them who will open up and develop the great wealth of both Palestine and Egypt.

The Great Pyramid will then become the controlling centre in the world's civilisation. Under their influence it will at last be fully explored,[1] the secret passage at present sealed up by the granite block in the side of what is called "the well" will at last be opened. Beneath the thirteen acre base of the Pyramid

[1] "Ephraim shall return to Egypt" (Hos. ix, 3).

a treasure temple will be discovered, one not only containing gold and jewels beyond the wildest dreams of imagination, but revealing scientific secrets by which the Pyramid was built, which will upset all previously known laws relating to Astronomy, gravitation, electricity, the harnessing of the powers of light, etheric rays and the hidden forces of the atom. With such knowledge at their disposal the Israelites and all the descendants of "the lost tribes" will become the possessors of the Earth in every sense as has been predicted so many times in the Bible.

That "the stranger" will be a co-worker with the returned Israelites in making Palestine and its surrounding counties the centre of a new and coming civilisation is clearly indicated in many pages of "the book." In Ezekiel's vision of the final restoration of the Israelites, and his description of the rebuilding of Jerusalem and the Temple, he distinctly states: "So shall ye divide this land among you according to the tribes of Israel . . . ye shall divide it by lot for an inheritance unto you *and to the strangers that sojourn among you,* which shall beget children among you; and they shall be *unto you as born in the country among the children of Israel;* they shall have *inheritance with you* among the tribes of Israel."[1]

[1]Ezek. xlvii, 21, 22.

Another Lawgiver, like Moses, will arise, who by grouping all nations under the significance of their Zodiacal signs, will cause wars between Nations to become impossible and so in the end through this "despised race" universal peace will become established.

Before this desired time can dawn, the great Armageddon must be fought. Where it will take place and the causes that will bring it about I will now endeavour to explain.

CHAPTER X

THE COMING WAR OF WARS

WHERE THE GREAT ARMAGEDDON WILL BE AND THE PROMISE OF UNIVERSAL PEACE

IN the mystery of Design, the "lost ten Tribes" have produced a somewhat similar effect that a dropped thread would do in the weaving of a large piece of tapestry. For the time being the picture may appear to be somewhat changed, the grand essentials of the plan may appear to be altered.

But the weaving goes on and on, as if nothing mattered. In the end, the lost thread seems to *have been purposely dropped,* the picture becomes more beautiful, more perfect, *and the design becomes so wonderful, in its clearness, that all may see its meaning.*

The "lost Tribes"—some millions of people were, we are told, "dispersed among the heathen." Later on the remaining two Tribes were driven out of Palestine and "scattered among the Gentiles," or as this word is "Goynin" in the Hebrew, it would be more correct to read this text as "scattered among the nations."

Such events in history did actually take place; of that there can be no shadow of doubt.

Was this part of some great and wonderful Design? I think of that also there can be no dispute. The "lost Tribes," like a purposely lost thread, will in the end make the Design the nearer to perfection.

The Israelites were most certainly "dispersed" exactly as had been prophesied some centuries before, but if "dispersed," they were not "lost"; they were *purposely blended and absorbed by other nations*, and this, it must be remembered, long before Christ was crucified.

Earlier in the preceding Chapters I have shown how the Israelites intermingled and intermarried with various races. Even such leaders as Joseph, Moses, and Solomon took unto them wives from other nations.

Is there any reason, therefore, to suppose that after the Ten Tribes were "dispersed" the main mass of this people did not also marry and become absorbed with other peoples such as the Phœnicians, Egyptians, Greeks, Slavs, Teutons, Gæls and Celts?

In long processes of time these wandering bands of Israelites, and their descendants who had intermarried with other nations, lost the essentials of their own religion and embraced the Pagan beliefs by which they were surrounded. Their former worship of the "Lord of Hosts" easily became the worship of the Sun God as the Lord of Life, but in all these forms of religion the mysterious influence of "the heavens" and the Twelve Houses of the Zodiac remained the paramount idea of whatever faith they adopted, as may be seen in the stone circles or "Waymarks" erected by them in their wanderings through various lands.

With the loss of their religion, the loss of the rite of Circumcision also had its effect and perhaps, in consequence, the features of the face, more especially the nose, became less and less marked, while climatic influences and diet also produced facial changes.

In this way the prophecies concerning the House of Israel, being "lost among the heathen," became fulfilled to the letter, even to the loss of their name, "And ye shall leave your name . . . for the Lord God shall call his servants by another name." (Isaiah lxv. 15.)

During all this long night of "dispersal" another section of this people appear to be just as purposely designated to carry on the old religion and tradition of their race.

The two Tribes of Judah and Levi who, after their return from the Babylonian Captivity to Jerusalem, received the name of Jews, after the final overthrow of Jerusalem and their dispersal among the Gentiles, clung to their religion and its rite of Circumcision with a tenacity that is without equal in the past history of races.

Persecuted with the utmost severity wherever they went, martyred by both Christian and Pagan, robbed, tortured and slaughtered by all, without land, home or Temple, they held to the religion of their fathers in spite of false Teachers and self-styled Messiahs who tempted them with "reforms" from time to time.

By the very bitterness of this persecution they have fulfilled the prophecies made regarding them.

"The Lord shall scatter thee among all people from the one end of the earth even unto the other, and among these nations shalt thou find no ease. And thy life shall hang in doubt before thee, and thou shalt fear day and night and have none assurance of thy life." (Deut. xxviii, 64, 65, 66.)

No other religion in the world survived such persecution or inspired and created so many other creeds. Egyptian worship existed for a long time, perhaps, five thousand years, and is now but a dream. From every corner of the earth monuments of past Faiths become to-day but tombstones of dead creeds. One religion alone, that of the Hebrews, has existed from the earliest ages of the world to the present day. Islam and Christianity are but modern faiths in comparison. Founded on the Laws of Nature in direct touch with the God of Nature, the commandments of Jehovah as he spake with Adam, Abraham, Isaac, Moses and the prophets, echo down the ages as fresh and full of truth as when, in the thunders of Sinai, the Ten Commandments were given for the foundation of all civilisations that have since followed.

In vain other races have tried to improve on "The Book" of the Hebrews. In vain Egyptians compiled their "Book of the Dead" or Islam followed with its Koran.

For two thousand years Church and State, Kings, Emperors, and colossal wealth have subsidised various religions—only to see them to-day split into a hundred sects with each one claiming a fragment of "the true Cross" as its own.

Since 1701 England alone has spent over one million pounds per year in Missionary work to convert "the heathen," with the result that Buddhist, Brahmin, Mohammedan, and Jew, after all these years, still outnumber Christians by some hundreds of millions.

In giving money for Missionary work Christians believe they are obeying the command of Christ, "Go ye unto all the world and preach the Gospel" forgetting that the meaning of the word Gospel is in reality "God's Spell" or "God's Truth," which is even more clearly set forth in the "Book of the Hebrews," the Old Testament, than in any other book that has ever been compiled.

The predicted period, "the Times of the Gentiles," is rapidly coming to its close; when it does, the outlines of Divine Design will appear and the reason for the "dispersal" of the Israelites and following them the Jews, will be made manifest. The Great Designer centuries ago has Himself said "The Lord thy God will turn thy captivity, and have compassion upon thee, and will return and gather thee from all the nations, whither the Lord thy God hath scattered thee." (Deut. xxx, 3.)

The Jews who for close on two thousand years have had no Country, no State, no Home, have been kept together by something no *other* race has had—namely a "Book," but one that contains their history—the records of prophecies that have been fulfilled and prophecies which they believe just as surely—*will be fulfilled.*

To no other race have such prophecies been made or such things accomplished, and so with confidence they look forward to the future. "He that scattered them will gather them" and in the "gathering" the "lost Tribes," the "dispersed" among the heathen, will be brought back *with those nations that have blended with them.* "For behold in those days and in that time . . . I will also gather *all nations* and will bring them down into the valley of Jehoshaphat, and will plead with them there for my people and for my heritage Israel, whom they have scattered among the nations, and parted my land." (Joel iii, 1, 2.)

We are told that "a thousand years are but a day in His sight" and for two thousand years the pattern and purpose of the Design has been slowly but surely filled in by the continual influence of the Jews in every country of the world. In spite of opposition, persecution and prejudice, the Israelite in all lands wherever he has wandered has kept "the Covenant" with the Creator that he would rest on the Sabbath Day and keep it holy. "Six days may work be done; but in the seventh is the sabbath of rest holy to the Lord . . . wherefore the Children of Israel shall . . . observe the Sabbath throughout their generations, *for a perpetual covenant.* It is a sign between me *and the children of Israel for ever.*" (Ex. xxxi, 15, 16, 17.)

In no matter what land the Jew has gone he has endeavoured to keep this Covenant, with the result that, as his influence spread through the world, "the heathen" have been compelled in spite of themselves to follow his example, and in consequence the seventh day —Saturday—is becoming more and more a day of rest in all countries where the Jew may be found.

As far back as the days of Josephus he relates "that in whatever lands the Jews settled the surrounding nations imitated their custom as to keeping of the seventh day as a day of rest." Coming nearer home we find that during the past fifty years all over Great Britain business premises either close early on Saturday or do not open at all. This custom has also spread rapidly over the United States of America and is recently becoming the general rule in all European countries wherever the Jews have become established.

Circumcision, which in Christian countries was principally only practised by the Jews, is now openly advocated by Medical men all over the world, and it will be remembered that in comparatively recent years the "seal of fashion" was stamped on it by King Edward the Seventh allowing it to be introduced to the Royal Household. On the Continent of Europe, in the United States of America and, in fact, all over the world, this custom is coming more and more into general practice.

Politically, the influence of the Jewish race is rapidly spreading in all countries. Up to Queen Victoria's reign no Jew could hold any office in the English Government. This was altered in the days of Disraeli when he became

Prime Minister of England, and to-day there is no position of power or distinction that a Jew may not hold—a recent example being in the case of Lord and Lady Reading holding the position of Viceroy and Vice-reine of India.

So many people misunderstand the Jew that they will, perhaps, disagree with me when I say that Finance is not the only walk in life that has a special claim upon his abilities. The real truth of the matter is that the Jew has been forced into finance by circumstances. During long years of persecution, it was the only position open to him; in order to exist he was compelled to buy and sell what "the heathen" made, he lent them money, he financed their enterprises, and having no country of his own he financed their wars, being more or less indifferent in the past as to what nation won or lost. After long centuries of practice in the manipulation of money he became naturally an expert in finance, and Finance becoming as it has done the principal power in the world, he to-day represents a force that is unequalled in shaping the destiny of mankind.

At the same time the Jew has also made himself felt in the world of Art, Literature, Music and Science, and with the greater freedom now dawning on his race there is no estimating what his future may not be along such lines.

The Jew is an adapter more than an inventor, he may not be found at the creation of Industries, but there is no one who knows better how to bring about combinations, groups and gigantic trusts. When the time comes he will exhibit this power in combinations of nations—and as he is to-day a man of peace rather than of war—his influence in the end will be to prevent war.

Before, however, this can take place, the Israelites as a race will be involved in the greatest conflict that has yet been known. The return to Palestine is what will bring this about.

This return to their land has been predicted for many centuries in "the Book," and as every prediction made about them in its pages has been fulfilled—so also, it is only logical to assume, will be their ultimate restoration in Palestine and the re-building of Jerusalem, the City of their Fathers.

"And it shall come to pass in the last days, that the mountain of the Lord's house shall be established . . . and all nations shall flow unto it. For out of Zion shall go forth the law, and the word of the Lord from Jerusalem." (Isaiah ii, 2-3.)

Some two hundred million acres of the richest land in the world, a country with splendid harbours and almost in the heart of Europe, has for close on two thousand years been lying waste as was prophesied, "the cities thereof shall be desolate, without any to dwell therein."[1]

All these things we know have taken place, and we are now seeing in our own day an equally steady and irresistible fulfilment of another set of prophecies made about this same race. We read that Jerusalem was to be trodden down under the feet of the Gentiles during "the Time of the Gentiles." We also know that a thousand years ago great Armies of Christians under the banner of the Crusaders attempted again and again to free this land. We have often wondered why the might and power behind "the Cross" could not drive out "the Crescent"; why with the blessing of "the Church" on all their efforts "the Armies of the Cross" always met with disaster. We perhaps did not realise that "the Times of the Gentiles" *had not been fulfilled*, that the Mohammedan Crescent was *also the servant of Destiny*, and the time had not come for the Gates of Jerusalem to be opened to an invading Army. Strange is it not to think that the same Cycle of years that appears to have played such an important rôle in this history of the House of Israel, the same 2,150 years would have so nearly to run its course before British troops with many Israelite soldiers and descendants of Israelites entered Jerusalem

[1] Jeremiah xlviii. 9.

under General Allenby in 1917. Since then for the first time in all these long two thousand years Jews can return to their country under British protection and *are returning year after year in astonishing numbers.*

Not only has it been prophesied that the Jews are to return to Palestine, but also the rest of the Ten Tribes. In Jer., chapter xxx, verse 3, we read, "I will bring again the captivity of my people Israel and Judah, saith the Lord: and I will cause them to return to the land that I gave their fathers, and they shall possess it," and again in Ezekiel, chapter xxxvii, verse 21, "I will take the children of Israel from among the heathen, whither they be gone, and *will gather them on every side, and bring them into their own land.*" And again in Amos x, 14, 15, "And they shall build the waste cities and inhabit them . . . and I will plant them upon their land, and they shall no more be pulled out of their land which I have given them, saith the Lord."

All these prophecies are being steadily fulfilled even to the union of Israel and Judah. To-day English, American, German and French capitalists are uniting with Jewish financiers to bring about a revival of prosperity in Palestine such as the world has never seen before. It is estimated that since the Great War over 150,000 Jews have returned and settled in Palestine.

I will now set out as briefly as possible my reasons for stating that the Armageddon yet to come will be brought about by the return of Judah and Israel to their country.

In the first place, Palestine and the surrounding countries will become the most fertile and one of the richest provinces in the world. Minerals and rare metals will be found there in abundance, and large deposits of coal and oil will be discovered in this part of the earth in inexhaustible quantities.[1]

As the ancient boundaries of Palestine originally extended to "the river of Egypt," so will the Israelites with their co-workers in Palestine open up Egypt which has been so closely associated with their history since long past ages. This development will arouse antagonism from the followers of Islam, and Turkey, backed by Russia, will endeavour to recapture Palestine.

In this coming War which is by no means far off, England will be attacked in all her Mohammedan possessions. She will give India her freedom, but religious warfare will rend that country from end to end until it becomes equally divided between the Mohammedan and the followers of Buddha. All her colonies will again send large numbers of men to help "the

[1] UNFATHOMED WEALTH OF THE DEAD SEA AND PALESTINE. £240,524,000,000.

Four great financial groups—British, American, European, and Anglo-Palestinian—are hankering after the concession to work

Mother country." Italy and Germany will at the same period be at war with France, and Spain under a Dictator will be engaged in a life and death struggle in North Africa. Germany and England will become allies and pour immense numbers of troops into Palestine and Egypt.

Russia will draw enormous masses of Chinese and Tartars with her and all Mohammedan races will be brought into the conflict.

The United States will be engaged in war with both Mexico and Japan and will not take part until later in the European carnage.

Great Britain will suffer terribly in the prolonged warfare, the most of London and Towns on the East Coast will be destroyed by fleets of aeroplanes from Russia.

---

the huge mineral and chemical deposits which lie hidden in the depths of the Dead Sea.

The imagination reels before the stupendous figures of the wealth estimated by the experts to be the value of the deposits. Here are a few of the plums of the Dead Sea fruit upon which the potential concessionaries are basing their calculations:

	Tons.	Value.
Potash	1,300,000,000	£14,000,000,000
Bromine	853,000,000	£52,000,000,000
Salt	11,900,000,000	£9,500,000,000
Gypsum	81,000,000	£25,000,000
Magnesium	22,000,000,000	£165,000,000,000
Total		£240,524,000,000

These figures are based upon current market prices.

This total represents an amount *equal to the aggregate income of Great Britain for* 100 *years.* And it is alluded to calmly by the experts as being a "reasonable estimate" of the wealth lying fallow in one of the most dreary, arid and desolate places of the earth's surface.

(Extract from newspapers 24th and 25th October, 1927.) ED.

In Ireland there will be Civil War between the North and South, and a new Irish Republic will inflict considerable damage by aeroplanes on such cities as Liverpool, Manchester, Birmingham, and the west of England.

This coming War although far greater and more terrible than the last, will be only one of the many that will occur in the next few hundred years leading up to the final Armageddon.

As foreshadowed in Ezekiel, chapter xxxviii, the great battle of Armageddon will be fought on the plains of Palestine. It is clearly set out for all those who may choose to read, that this conflict will be a life and death struggle for the contending armies fighting in Palestine. It describes that the people of the North, by which Russia is evidently indicated, will descend into that country "with allies drawn from Persia, Ethiopia, Libya and many people." Ezekiel goes on to say, speaking of the Ruler or King of the North, and describing in unmistakable language the new conditions in Palestine caused by the return of the Israelites, "It shall come to pass, that at the same time shall things come into thy mind, and thou shalt think an evil thought: And thou shalt say, I will go to *the land of unwalled villages*; I will go *to them that are at rest* (namely to the Israelites returned from their long wanderings) . . . to take a spoil, and to take a prey; to turn thine hand upon *the des-*

olate places that are now inhabited, and upon the people that are *gathered out of the nations*. . . . And thou shalt come from thy place out of the north parts, thou, and many people with thee . . . and thou shalt come up against my people of Israel, as a cloud to cover the land."[1]

At first the prophet indicates that the people from the North are likely to be successful; he then proceeds to describe how the Lord of Hosts will come to the aid of His people by earthquake, storm, flood, fire and plague. Then he goes on to say that the Lord will give unto "Gog" as he calls the people from the North, "a place there of graves in Israel . . . and there shall they bury Gog and all his multitude: and they shall call *it* the Valley of Hamon-gog. . . And they shall sever out men of continual employment, passing through the land to bury those that remain upon the face of the earth, to cleanse it . . . and when any seeth a man's bone, then shall he set up a sign by it, till the buriers have buried it in the Valley of Hamon-gog. Then shall they (Israel) know I am the Lord their God, which caused them to be led into captivity among the heathen: but I have gathered them unto their own land, and have left none of them any more there."[2]

[1] Ezekiel xxxviii, verses 5, 15, 16.
[2] Ezekiel xxxix, verses 11, 15, 21, 28.

CHAPTER XI

THE COMING AQUARIAN AGE AND THE EMANCIPATION OF WOMAN

WOMEN IN POLITICS, IN BUSINESS AND IN FREEMASONRY

THE first vibrations of what is called the New Aquarian Age, caused by the "Precession of the Equinoxes" entering the Sign of Aquarius, commenced, roughly speaking, about the year A.D. 1762.

This sign of the Zodiac, more immediately influenced as it is by the Planets Uranus and Saturn, has, in the minds of ancient students of Occultism from time immemorial, been associated with the idea of "a new age" and complete change in the laws controlling civilisation. It was believed and understood that the peculiar vibrations caused by the action of the Sun retrograding through this part of the Zodiac would *so affect the minds of humanity that the most astounding changes, upheavals, and revolutions would follow in its train.*

The Aquarian period of 2,150 years, which we are now commencing, has been called "the new Age" by various schools of philosophy on account of the influence of Uranus being the first planet outside the zone of the earth's immediate rulers, and one that appears to have a distinctly different revolution like that of Neptune, which are the only two planets that in Occult symbolism affect *the thoughts* of individuals more than *the material.*

The "Aquarian" or "New Age" has also been set down as the period when woman in the order of upheaval, revolution, and change, would appear on the world's stage in a completely new rôle.

A retrospective glance over the events of the past century and a half will be enough to show that great changes have already taken place in the mental outlook of humanity at large, *and more particularly so in the position of women.*

Up to this period, for thousands of years, women in all lands have been mere chattels, in a state of serfdom little better than slaves, without any voice in the making of laws that affected them.

Since the commencement of this "New Age" no changes have been more marked *than that of the position of women in all countries of the world.*

Even in such old civilisations as China and Japan, in spite of the most rock-bound laws of dynasties and religions, women have everywhere thrown off their shackles.

In Japan, up to as recently as 1910, no actress was allowed on the stage, and all feminine rôles had to be taken by men. Women were not allowed by law to appear on the stage in any capacity.

Since 1910 all this has been altered, some famous Japanese actresses have even visited Europe, and still more recently the daughters of Japan's highest nobility have appeared on the stage.[1]

In Turkey, for the first time in centuries, the doors of the Harem have been opened, women have torn the veil and "the yashmak" from their faces, and appear openly among the public.

During the French Revolution in 1793, women fought behind the barricades in Paris side by side with their brothers. In the last Great War Russian women formed themselves into regiments, and entered the trenches as bravely as men. To-day under Soviet rule women are encouraged to enter the Army and have entered it in large numbers.

Coming nearer home we find that France recently passed an Act to conscript women into Military Service in the event of another War.

It is only a short time ago when women, and some of them members of England's high-

[1] The daughter of Baron Sanji Narahara has joined the Geijutsu Theatre in Tokio. (See Public Press, November, 1927.—Ed.)

est aristocracy, marched through the streets of London under Suffragette banners, went to prison and endured "hunger-strikes" in their fight for "equal rights with men."[1]

To-day they go one step farther and demand the vote at the age of twenty-one, which demand will be granted before long, just assuredly as the night must follow the day.[2]

Women scientists, women doctors, women barristers, women preachers, and women chauffeurs, have come to stay. Women have swum the Channel, have steered Aeroplanes, and invaded every occupation that man at one time thought exclusively his own.

Women's clubs have sprung up all over the world. In America they have become so powerful that no political issue can succeed without their support.

Women have been elected as Governors of States, as Mayors of Towns, and during the next fifty years a woman President will undoubtedly occupy the White House at Washington.

In England the trend of events is flowing in the same direction. Women have already entered Parliament, and have become members of the Cabinet, and still later a Queen will again sway the destinies of Britain.

Even the Church is weakening before the influence of woman. Bishops bow their heads

[1] 1910 to 1914. [2] Act of Parliament passed in 1928.

to her desires, and Vicars owe their "livings" to her hands. Civil Marriages that a few years ago were anathema in the eyes of priests are to-day "blessed" by a subsequent service.

Women have flouted the authority of the "Church" by creating creeds of their own. Mrs. Baker Eddy founded "Christian Science" which, in spite of opposition and prejudice, has spread to every country of the globe. Mrs. Annie Besant, preaching the cult of Theosophy, has a position in India and the East as powerful as any Pope. In the West of America Mrs. Kathrine Tingley up to the time of her death in 1930, under another banner of Theosophy reigned as a spiritual Queen, while Aimée McPherson of Los Angeles with her "Foursquare Gospel" can number her followers by hundreds of thousands.

Since the dawn of this "New Age" there is nothing that man has held sacred that women have not in the last century and a half demanded as their right. Even the secrets of Freemasonry have not escaped. As this "New Age" commenced to dawn across the world woman presented herself for admittance—and to a certain measure has already crossed the portals.

In 1775, according to the writings of Monsieur Boubée, one of the authorities on Freemasonry on the Continent, "the French ladies not wishing to remain indifferent to the good done by Freemasons, sought to form Lodges of Adoption, so as the more efficiently to exercise Charity and Goodness." We read that the Grand Lodge of France eventually consented to these Lodges being formed on the express understanding that "*each Meeting should be presided over by the Master of a regular Masonic Lodge.*"

Among the distinguished ladies who were enrolled in these Lodges were Princesse de Lamballe, Comtesse de Polignac, the Duchesse de Chartres, the Duchesse de Bourbon, the Comtesse de Choiseul and the Marquis de Coutebonne.

On the 11th March, 1775, the Marquis de Saisseval with other distinguished Freemasons founded one of these Lodges for women *under* the constitution of the Grand Lodge of France. At the opening ceremony the Duchesse de Chartres, the wife of the Grand Master, was present, and the Duchesse de Bourbon agreed to take the position of Grand Mistress of Adoptive Masonry. Her installation took place the next day, at which the Duc de Chartres, as Grand Master of French Freemasons, presided. It is related that upwards of a thousand persons, the highest of the nobility of France, were present.

On the 20th March, 1785, records show that Marie Antoinette's most intimate friend, the Princesse de Lamballe, was elected to the position of Grand Mistress of Honour in a Lodge founded by the famous Cagliostro, called the "Egyptian rite." The magnificence of that ceremony of her installation surpassed everything that had been done before and the most prominent Freemasons, together with some of the highest members of the Court of Louis XVI, were present.[1]

Pope Clement the XII in 1730 issued his Bull against Freemasonry, but, in spite of this, women's Lodges continued to flourish on the Continent.

Napoleon the First gave his patronage to Lodges for women, and in 1805 Monsieur Boubée writes the Empress Josephine was installed as Grand Mistress of the "Lodge Imperial." At no period in the history of Adoptive Masonry, he tells us, "were so many distinguished persons present to witness the installation of a Sovereign."

In England after the execution of Charles the First, who had been initiated into Masonry by Ashmole, his widow founded a Masonic Society for women, under the name of "The Children of the Widow," which all Freemasons have a right to call themselves.

About the year 1778 an Order for women called the "Eastern Star" was founded in the United States; although this order does not claim to come under the jurisdiction of

[1] *Histoire de la Magie*, par P. Christian.

Freemasonry it is decidedly Masonic in its foundation, and when opportunity offers, holds its meetings in regular Freemasons' temples. It is the largest Order for women in the world and numbers over one million in its membership. As well as this Order for women there is another very important organisation called the Order of Co-Masons, who have many lodges in America and in England.

The Honourable Fraternity of Ancient Masonry, another organisation for women, is spreading rapidly in London and the Provinces. At the moment of writing it has upwards of nine Lodges in active operation in London.

In speaking of this organisation in a paper read before the Lodge of Installed Masters in Birmingham in October, 1925, F. W. G. Gilby, a Past Provincial Grand Chaplain, praises most highly this order of women Freemasons. He says: "This Order is pure and well-worked Masonry. I was Grand Chaplain of the Order for some years and learned much. . . . It was this order which in the year 1920 presented a petition to Grand Lodge for examination with a view to recognition. They did not ask that women should be admitted to men's lodges; they did not desire that. They only asked for this examination that the *status quo ante* might be restored, and that Masons who are under the jurisdiction of Grand Lodge might not be debarred from visiting the lodges of their particular Order, which is the nearest in practice to our own."[1]

The United Grand Lodge of England refused the petition to grant recognition to women's Lodges, but in spite of that decision the movement in favour of women creating their own Masonic organisations is going on apace.

Considering the advances made by women in all countries of the world and the positions they have won in the face of opposition of the most conservative bodies of men, and knowing that "the New Age" we are now commencing is a predestined period of time in which women have to come to the front in all matters of public life, I have no hesitation in saying that there is no body of men who will be able for long to resist the tide of thought that for either good or evil is bringing women into power.

It may be that the revolutions and upheavals we see around us on all sides may for the time being bring about the fall of Empires, the destruction of Thrones, the death of the "old" and the birth of the "new." It may be that times of great tribulations lie in store for humanity—I am however such

[1] *Women and Freemasonry*, by F. W. G. Gilby, M.A., Past Provincial Grand Chaplain, Warwick.

a believer in the ultimate perfection of Divine Design that I see in the symbol of the Aquarian Age the promise of "the Water Bearer" pouring out water on the earth, that in the end seeds may have more richness, flowers more fullness and all sections of humanity more love for one another.

As we are alas, only now, on what may be called the "cusp" of the Aquarian precession many hundreds of years must pass before humanity will begin to feel its beneficial effects.

In the meanwhile there will be many "Great Wars" until the final Armageddon—the War of Wars—that will end War.

sign of the Zodiac into another. It can be proved by all astronomers who wish to make these calculations that the exact point of the Vernal Equinox in the year 388 B.C. was in the first degree of the sign of Aries and that it had *left the Sign of Taurus* 2,150 years before that date. The next sign in this movement of "the precession" after Aries is that of the Sign of Pisces, the symbol of the fishes in which Christ appeared and the new religion of Christianity commenced. Therefore in the year 388 B.C. "the Precession of the Equinox" was retrograding from Aries into the Sign of Pisces and the following calculation will enable us to know our present position.

If one adds 388 B.C. to the year, 1931, we obtain 2,319, deduct from this the 2,150 years of "the precession" it leaves 169 years, and we therefore know that we are at the present time 169 years in the sign following Pisces, namely, Aquarius—and that the "Cusp" of the new Aquarian Age is even now upon us.

Deduct 169 years from 1931 and we are back in A.D. 1762, a period when very marked changes were taking place in the world. About this date a new nation, the United States, was *being* born; fourteen years later her Declaration of Independence was issued. In Europe great changes were taking place. France was steadily going forward to the revolution that shook the Thrones of Monarchy, from which they have never recovered.

Napoleon was being born (1769), the demons of war were drunk with blood, and all Europe turned into a battlefield. The power of Rome was shaken to its foundations, her churches robbed, her priests expelled from France (1793).

Saturn, ruler of the sign Aquarius, is only at the commencement of his reign. War, destruction, bloodshed, and famine are the instruments of his purpose—the tools by which he destroys convention and enthrones "the new" on the ruins of the old.

We are only at the beginning—the commencement of things—a little over a hundred years across the threshold, a mere nothing in the 2,150 years of the Aquarian Age that is coming.

Just as there is a "Cusp" in the ordinary year of seven days as the Sun passes from one Sign of the Zodiac into another, during which the preceding Sign overlaps the next, so there is in the "Great Year of the Precession" 700 years of its larger "Cusp" before the "precess" is fully accomplished, as we are only 169 years over the commencement of the "Cusp" of the coming Sign of Aquarius. We have therefore 531 years from our present date to pass through before the World is fully in the Aquarian Age.

The coming five hundred odd years will be a period of upheaval in every sense of the term, breaking up of Empires, birth of new Nations, Revolutions and Wars, leading up to the Great Armageddon, which will take place about five hundred years from now.

From another point of view the change that the Axis of the Earth is slowly and steadily undergoing as each "precess" of the Equinox makes its effect, has in the past, and must in the future, cause equally important changes in the climatic conditions of each country.

As the equilibrium of the centre of the globe becomes altered great earthquakes will take place in all parts of the world until the Earth-crust will again become settled and normal. From now on, severe earth-tremors and quakes will affect countries which have been more or less immune from such occurrences. Extinct volcanoes all over the world will become active, while tidal waves and cyclones will cause enormous destruction to property.

During the coming 50 years an earthquake zone will develop in a North Easterly direction from the Pacific Coast of Peru, passing through Panama and Mexico, through the Northern States and Canada to the Arctic regions.

Eastern Cities of North America such as Washington, New York, Buffalo, Boston and

Toronto, will be seriously affected and a considerable part of New York will be destroyed. A new ridge or belt of land will appear in the North Atlantic which will so cause the Gulf Stream to alter its course that the Eastern States of America will become subjected to intensely cold winters, and the Glacial Age will by degrees be repeated in Northern Europe; such countries as Ireland, Great Britain, Sweden, Norway, Denmark, the north parts of Russia, Germany, France and Spain will gradually become uninhabitable.

This alteration will be compensated by the development of a temperate climate affecting such countries as China, India, Africa, and Egypt, and in consequence a rapid increase of civilisation will be the result in all these countries.

During the next fifty to a hundred years after a series of devastating earthquakes, the islands of the Azores will rise from the Atlantic and the ruins of the long lost continent of Atlantis will be discovered and explored.

This upheaval of the ocean bed will break the Isthmus of Panama, North and South America will become two immense islands and enormous trade will develop through this route.

There are many persons who believe that the original submersion of Atlantis caused the Atlantic Ocean to burst through "the Pillars of Hercules" at Gibraltar and turn a once fertile valley into what is now known as the Mediterranean Sea. The reappearance of Atlantis will, in this latter case, cause the Sahara Desert to be transformed into a huge inland sea and so cause such climatic changes on the continent of Africa that the present arid wastes of the Northern parts of that country, together with Egypt, will be transformed into a temperate zone of such richness that Palestine, Egypt, and the surrounding countries will become the granaries of the world and will make of this portion of the globe a great centre of civilisation.

In a period of about five hundred years from now, the aftermath of the Great Armageddon will completely revolutionise our present ideas of nations, kingdoms or republics; a wonderfully organised Central Government in Palestine will radiate laws of life and humanity to the entire world.

After their long trials and persecutions the restored House of Israel and Judah, having learned so much from their own sufferings, will be in a position to appreciate the wrongs of other races, and will adjust these wrongs by the Balance of Divine Justice.

Despised peoples will be given an equal chance with those who up to now have been the most favoured. Just as in far gone ages when the sons of Joseph born in Egypt from an Egyptian wife were brought into the sacred circle of the Twelve Tribes, so the children of Ishmael and the sons of Ham will become recognised, and the Negro, the Arab, the Hindu, and the Yellow race, instead of being regarded as an enemy or a "peril" will be drawn into universal co-partnership whose purpose will be the uplifting of the entire human race *and the fulfilment of the Divine Design whose ultimate purpose is the perfection of all.*

Such perfection cannot be attained until all religions have become merged into one. This, the apparently "impossible," is every day becoming more and more probable. The sway and power of State-supported creeds is on the decline, or splitting into so many sects that they are "like sheep without a shepherd." The Commandment "Thou shalt have no other Gods before me" still rings out as clear to-day as it did on Sinai, "the *heavens* declare the glory of God" in this age as they did when He created Twelve Tribes to be emblematic of the Twelve Houses of the Zodiac, and instituted a Temple to be made "according to the pattern shown in the heavens." The Voice that said, "Oh Israel thou hast sinned even from the days of Gibeah" when the mysterious covenant and law of "twelve" was broken for the first time, still holds the promise to all humanity "I will be thy God and thou shalt be my people." The "religion of the heavens" is still the only religion by which God "talks with man" to-day as He did in the days of old. In the light of such knowledge, all mysteries will be made plain, God's message written across the heavens will in the end become correctly interpreted, the language of stars, planets, and suns, will translate "the Book" into words "understandable by the people." Nations will so realise their Zodiacal affinities that they will group themselves together and the unnatural frontiers of the present day will be swept away. Under such conditions war will become impossible and the "promise of peace" will at last be fulfilled. "They shall beat their swords into plough-shares, and their spears into pruning-hooks: nation shall not lift up sword against nation, neither shall they learn war any more." (Isaiah ii, 4.)

PART II

PREDICTIONS CONCERNING THE IMMEDIATE FUTURE OF THE PRINCIPAL NATIONS OF THE WORLD

First Series:

GREAT BRITAIN AND BRITISH COLONIES IN GENERAL

HIS Majesty King George V, on the 3rd of June 1931, completed the third cycle of seven, namely, twenty-one years on the Throne of England.

From an astrological point of view the new cycle he now enters will be a very serious and critical one, both for him as King of England and as a physical human being.

When I first published this book in 1927, on page 68 I stated: "The planetary influence governing King George will be unfavourable for him personally between 1928 and 1930. I foresee in those years, a critical time and a period of deep anxiety for the Royal Family and the British Empire as a whole." This came truc by his serious illness which commenced in November, 1928, and ran through the following year of 1929. A drainage operation had to be performed on his lung; this critical condition lasted until the middle of 1930.

His condition was so serious that it will be remembered the Prince of Wales was recalled from his tour in South Africa and forced to return to England. It was a period of the deepest anxiety for not only the Royal Family and England, but for all the far-flung British Possessions in all parts of the World.

From this extremely serious illness His Majesty recovered.

I am sorry to have to state that although His Majesty has resumed his regular duties and has been in such good health that he was able to attend the Royal Derby dinner in the Spring of 1931, I have grave fears of a recurrence of ill health for him between October and December of this year. Unless the greatest precautions are taken, the most serious results may be anticipated.

The position of both Saturn and Mars is so menacing, both for King George and for England generally, that the most far-reaching effects can only be expected.

It would be well if His Majesty's Advisors compelled him to leave England before the end of September, 1931, to winter abroad in the South of Europe. But against the probability of His Majesty doing so, must be taken the serious conditions coming on in

England, which may force the King to remain at his post of duty and so compel him to fit in with the design of Destiny.

Even what is called the "fadic" numbers made by the name and title of King George V, works out to the compound number of 14, which produces in itself the simple digit of 5. This number I explained very fully in my Book of Numbers on page 18[1]. The year 1931, if added together, produces the number of 14 for its compound and 5 for its single digit; this, in itself, foreshadows that the year containing that number will have a peculiar effect on His Majesty's life.

In publishing this book several years ago, I wrote: "Born on June 3, in the Zodiacal sign of Gemini, called the 1st House of Air, accentuates the dangers foreshadowed by the compound number of the name and title of King George V. Therefore, his greatest danger will come from anything in connection with air; even His Majesty's lungs, as the breathing apparatus of his system, comes under this symbol of the Zodiacal sign of birth."

In His Majesty's Horoscope cast for the moment of birth, June 3rd, 1865 at 1.18 A.M., at Marlborough House, London, the sign of Capricorn (House of Saturn) is placed at the zenith or highest point of his Horoscope, making Saturn exalted and angular.

[1] "Cheiro's Book of Numbers Vols. I and II."

This is of singular significance for the year 1931, both for the King and for England as a Nation, as from the commencement of the year Saturn will be the most exalted and powerfully placed planet in the heavens, with bad aspects from Uranus and Mars as far as Great Britain is concerned.

Furthermore Saturn will afflict all Countries that come under his influence, especially India; a point I will go into more fully when I come to write about that country.

Her Majesty Queen Mary, during 1931, also comes under the evil influences of Saturn and Mars. Her own health will be afflicted and a very anxious time in every way appears lying directly ahead of her.

Illness and death of a member of the Royal Family is indicated to take place about the Summer or Autumn of 1931.

Before the Prince of Wales, also, will lie a very active and important year. He will be called on to take part in missions to other countries, to take long voyages, and towards the Autumn, a journey in the direction of North America, Canada or the United States may be projected. I would, however, strongly advise him not to be away from England towards the end of 1931.

Some important event concerning either Prince Henry or Prince George, may be expected before the termination of 1931, which will bring either one or the other, or both into the light of publicity.

Both 1931 and 1932 will be two of the most marked years in connection with the Royal Family of England.

England as a Nation and the Government at Westminster.

There is nothing very favourable that I can foresee for England,—the home country —or for Great Britain in general.

The overwhelming downfall of the Conservative Party, and the Labour Party's taking over the helm of Government on May 31st 1929, marked an epoch in the history of Great Britain of the most far-reaching importance. The last action of the previous Conservative Government in giving the vote to women from the age of twenty-one was suicidal as far as the Conservative Party was concerned and placed the political situation in the hands of Labour.

Women and girls employed in the thousands of English factories used the power placed in their hands to vote for the section they belonged to, namely, that of Labour.

Astrologically it was the wrong time to make such a drastic change, with the planets of Saturn and Mars in such a menacing position.

The influence of Saturn has, from time immemorial, been considered to bring about restrictions and privations of all kinds. In connection with the destiny of countries, it brings about loss of trade, tightness of money, failure of crops, lack of employment and such like evils.

The opposition of Saturn to Jupiter from January 10th, 1931 makes the outlook still worse and reduces all promise of any immediate improvement.

Jupiter, called the planet of expansion, is completely over-ruled by the bad aspects from both Saturn and Mars. Consequently, instead of "expansion," one can only look forward to "restriction" in every sense of the word, with the attendant threatened danger that war, revolution and bloodshed may also, during the coming two years, involve England, either at home or abroad.

The conjunction of Saturn with Mercury which commenced in January, 1931, will be evil for trade and commerce generally for Great Britain as well as other countries and will accentuate trade depression.

The Labour Government, although attacked on every side, will hold its own for some time; and should any appeal be made to the country, the Labour Party will be returned to power stronger than ever.

Taxation will increase in England and new methods will be devised by the Labour Government to meet its ever-increasing deficit.

Communism and Socialism will increase rapidly during the coming years and mysterious fires and destruction will result.

A wave of dissatisfaction and unrest will make itself manifest in many sections of the Army and Navy, and the British Air force during 1930 and 1931 will be under evil influences, and will meet with unexpected disasters and heavy loss of life.[1]

Travel by Air generally will be under these bad conditions in almost all countries and some terrible tragedies of the air will take place.

At the same time some extraordinary developments in Air travel, together with new inventions relating to it may be expected.

A new non-inflammable gas will shortly make its appearance; and a different type of engine will revolutionize airships of all kinds.

Mars and Neptune forming a conjunction on June 16, 1931, threaten unusual unrest among workers in England generally, involving strikes of a revolutionary nature, increased unemployment and an unprecedented wave of lawlessness and crime. On account of the slow moving planets Uranus and Saturn,

[1] This commenced with the mysterious explosion, with heavy loss of life, of the great British Airship in the Spring of 1931.

and their important position in connection with the destiny of Great Britain, these bad conditions will last for a very long time.

This period will commence a still more difficult cycle in England's relations with India than any that has been in the past. (I will go into this more fully when I come to write on India in later pages.)

English railways from now on will commence a period of unfavourable conditions unequalled in their history. They will lose both passenger and freight traffic in every part of their system. In the next few years, even the great Mail Lines will be on the verge of bankruptcy and the Government will be forced to come to their assistance.

Under financial stringency they will be unable to keep their lines and rolling stock in proper repair and disastrous accidents will be continually on the increase.

Many of the Railway Companies will reduce dividends to their shareholders and some cease paying altogether.

English Shipping Interests will, from now on, be equally adversely affected, foreign trade becoming more and more restricted. Shareholders will be in a bad way and many reconstructions of Companies take place.

During 1931 and the Spring of 1932, some large shipping disaster is likely to occur

Also a mysterious explosion on some large English Battleship and the loss of some of the largest submarines.[1]

During this period storms and gales of unusual force will ravage the coasts of the British Isles; great damage to property will be the result, together with a heavy toll of shipping and lives.

In previous predictions I made the statement that Countries which had formerly been immune from earthquakes and earth-subsidences, would, from the year 1926, suffer considerably from such things.

In the Publisher's Preface to this book, the Editor bears testimony that I predicted, nine months in advance, the earthquake that took place in the Channel Islands in July, 1926, which "would be followed by another over a large area of England in the Autumn of the same year"; which will still be remembered in the Midlands. I also wrote that, from that date on, similar shocks would be felt in England, Northern France and Germany, especially during the years of 1931 and 1932.[2]

[1] June 12, 1931 (Universal Service) announced "suspension of diving operation to raise the British submarine Poseidon sunk off the Chinese Coast. The eighteen members of the crew trapped on the vessel are believed dead."

[2] Newspapers of June 7, 1931, reported that an earthquake took place that morning in the North Sea, fifty miles off the coast, that was felt all over England, and from Norway to the centre of France, and was the worst earthquake in that region for over one thousand years.

During 1931 a shipping combine will be made between England and Germany which will lead to some startling developments. About the same time Great Britain and Germany will come together on a closer relationship which will cause unpleasantness and friction with France. This arrangement will be greatly to the advantage of the two former countries.

As I stated previously in "Cheiro's World Predictions" page 38; "England, Germany, Denmark, Western Poland, Palestine, Syria and Japan are governed by the Sign of Aries, with Mars as ruler of that sign; it is inevitable that these countries must sooner or later be drawn together and intermingle in one another's affairs."

A combination of these countries is likely to take place during 1931 and 1932. It is advisable that it should take place, as if it did it might put off or delay war in Europe that is decidedly threatening.

I foresee a "working alliance" for self-preservation that, before long, will take place between Russia, Germany and Italy. Through the short-sightedness of her rulers, England may be left out of this powerful combine; if so, she would again miss a wonderful opportunity for her own security and advancement.

This "lost opportunity" is quite likely to happen owing to the prejudice that exists against Russia in the minds of some of the important Ministers of the Government of England, which might prevent any treaty or combination bringing Great Britain, Russia, Germany and Italy into a combine or alliance. So it is that the personal views of one man or another fit into, or play almost unknowingly, the game that Fate has prepared in advance.

Against the above combination, the position of France must be considered. France has, at the present time, the largest and most powerful Army in all Europe; with an Air Force that is unrivalled in its numbers, training and up-to-date methods. She recently prevented the Naval Agreement between the Great Powers becoming an actuality, for the simple reason that she would not allow Italy to possess a Navy as powerful as her own.

Still more recently, in the Spring of 1931, she has waxed wroth at the idea of Germany and Austria forming a commercial treaty to reduce tariffs between the two countries.

France is, therefore, not likely to allow a combine between Russia, Germany and Italy to eventuate if she can possibly prevent it.

Shortly after the Great War she, herself, formed a treaty of alliance with the weak states of Roumania and what is called the "little Entente," which always has and always will be "the powder-mine of Europe."

France is pledged, by her treaty, to go, with Military assistance, to the aid of any one of these smaller nations should they be attacked by any other power.

At the Treaty of Versailles, after the War, the representatives of the fourteen victorious nations sat round a long table and allowed themselves to be dictated to by the late President Wilson of the United States. As all the nations were heavily in debt to America, they were as subservient as debtors usually are under such circumstances.

President Wilson, although an extremely well-meaning man, was about as ignorant of the real conditions of Europe as any man could possibly be. He had no training in the age-long jealousies, rivalries, under-ground ambitions and perpetual bickerings of the countries whose maladies he was so suddenly called on to treat.

Like a doctor at a consultation table, every symptom that could be imagined was laid before his spectacled eyes. (No wonder the strain on his nervous system became so great that he returned to die shortly afterwards in his own country.)

He was told by the political butchers around the Conference table, that a drainage tube had to be inserted in the intestines of Poland to give her an exit to the sea. He agreed on "the Polish Corridor," not considering that such a "drainage tube" was schemed by the "butchers" to cut through the vitals of Germany and weaken that nation still further.

He lost sight of the natural law—that after an operation, parts cut asunder must, sooner or later, make an effort to join together and that until they do, *an open sore* is usually the result.

He was told that Roumania had to be compensated because her Oil Wells were blown up by her Allies, but a slice cut off the belly of the Great Bear—Russia, would balance matters.

President Wilson had never studied bears, so he let the "butchers" do the cutting. The "butchers" did the cutting in an unusually clumsy manner; the slice they cut off was the enormous province of Bessarabia. This piece of the belly of the Great Bear they presented to Roumania, forgetting that bears have unusual recuperative powers and that, sooner or later, it might recover and demand that piece of its lost stomach *for its own digestive purposes.*

Roumania got more than she could swallow and has been ill ever since.

France received back the rich provinces of Alsace-Lorraine, with heavy reparation charges. England got the German colonies, together with German battleships. Italy, although she joined up late, was given large portions of Austria. America was promised she would get back all the money she had lent, with added interest.

The "political butchers" were satisfied; they had done a wonderful piece of carving —*they thought.* Wise men—so wise they could not see they had carved for themselves a greater war than ever, in the coming future. And the tragedy of it all! Millions of lives thrown away for nothing. Millions of peoples impoverished for ages, all for the Treaty of Versailles; a piece of paper that will yet go down to posterity as the "Treaty of Folly."

SCOTLAND AND WALES

Since "Cheiro's World Predictions" were published in 1927, I have received a large number of letters asking me, in this revised edition, to give some information as to the future indications for Scotland and Wales.

It gives me much pleasure in answering these requests.

Scotland is governed in the Zodiac by the Sign of Cancer; its planets are the Moon and Neptune, suitable in every sense when one considers that the word "Scot" means the "Wanderer."

The sons and daughters of Scotland have

wandered to every part of the known world. They make excellent Colonists and are welcomed in every land to which they go.

The Scotch people, taken as a class, are an extremely patient, long-suffering race, which is also to be expected when one considers that the opposite Sign to Cancer, in the Zodiac, is Capricorn, with its ruler Saturn.

Perhaps, for this reason, they have put up with burdens and grievances that no other race would have borne so patiently.

Ireland, under the sign of Taurus (The Bull), has bellowed forth her troubles till the whole world has heard of her "wrongs," and as Ireland has, in the opposite point of the Zodiac, the Sign of Scorpia, otherwise called the second House of Mars, Ireland has never given up in the fight for her independence, and never will.

It may surprise many of my readers to know that Scotland broods under many grievances against England, although she has not let the world know very much about them.

The "Stone of Destiny" upon which her Kings had been crowned for more than 800 years, to which I have alluded in an earlier chapter of this book, was taken from her by Edward the First and carried to London in 1298, but it is not so generally known that after the battle of Bannockburn in 1314, in the Treaty made by England, she promised that the Stone of Destiny would be returned to Scotland.[1] This promise was never kept.

In the Treaty of Union in 1707 there were many other pledges made by England to Scotland that were also never fulfilled, but it would make this book too long if I were to attempt to go into the details here.

Looking back over the pages of history it is interesting to notice that both the Scotch and the Irish fought out their grievances against England on the battlefields of France.

It was the Scots who went to the aid of the French before the time of Joan of Arc when, with 12,000 men, they beat the English troops at the battle of Beaugé. It is also interesting to realise that seven hundred hardy Scots formed a body-guard to Joan of Arc.

In later years the Irish had their revenge for their broken Treaty of Limerick by defeating the English at the battle of Fontenoy.

There was no British Empire before the Treaty of Union with Scotland in 1707.

Without the Scots there might never have been an Empire, for the Scottish race have always been the Pioneers of Britain;

[1] Treaty of Northampton, 1314.

it is to them England owes the colonisation of Canada and the opening up of South Africa and Australia.

Coming down to recent history and the more immediate grievances under which Scotland suffers, we find that this country has been given no place in the League of Nations, also she has no representative on the Imperial Conference, whereas Ireland has obtained no less than five.

No separate return of Scotland's revenue position has been issued by England since 1921. In the years 1920–21 Scotland paid in Taxes to the British Government, £119,753,000. She received back for Scottish Services only £33,095,000; the balance remained in England. Perhaps this may account for the fact, before stated, that no separate return of Scotland's revenue position *has been issued since* 1921.

This certainly is a grievance. If it had happened to Ireland the whole world would have heard of it long before now.

Scottish Railways have been absorbed by English Companies and the greater part of repair work is now done in English workshops.

Scottish Banks are little more than branches of English Banks and the Bank of England controls them all.

Scotland has no less than one-fifth of her soil given over to Deer Forests and sporting rights principally owned and exploited by Dukes and Lords, or rented out by them to visiting American millionaires.

Scotland's population is *steadily decreasing*, as shown by the returns for recent years.

Scotland's unemployment is actually *sixteen per cent worse than England's*.

But you have read enough. Is there any hope of improvement, you ask? From an Astrological standpoint I truthfully cannot say there is. Things might improve if Scotland had her own Government and managed her own affairs; but knowing the patient nature of the Scots, I think such an event will be a long time in coming.

WALES

Wales, has always been considered under the influence of the Zodiacal Sign of Gemini, with its ruler the planet Mercury (positive). This fittingly describes the temperament and qualities of the Welsh people, taking them as a whole.

The attributes of the Sign of Gemini, (the First House of the Triplicity of Air), are, as a rule, more mental than physical.

People under this Sign of the Zodiac can be described as more *clever* than intellectual. Quick witted and quick in thought and action, they make the most of their opportunities and generally outdistance their more "tortoise-like" rivals.

Wales is coming under more favourable planetary conditions than any other part of Great Britain; especially in matters concerned with electric inventions or the practical utilisation of electricity.

Under these good aspects I foresee some great development coming on in this country, for the greater use of her rivers or waterfalls for the production of cheap electric power. It may be that the dream of harnessing the tides of the Severn will become a reality and so cause Wales to become a great manufacturing centre.

Some new invention in connection with the manufacture of fuel and the reduction of waste from Coal mines is also likely in the next few years to be demonstrated by this country's coal fields.

THE IRISH FREE STATE AND NORTHERN IRELAND

Northern Ireland, remaining as it has done, as a part of Great Britain, under the Government of Westminster, will be influenced by the same conditions that I indicated for England.

The Ascent of Belfast, the capital of Northern Ireland, is 14·50 degrees of Leo;

the Ascendant of London is 17·10 degrees of Leo.[1] Whether one takes this calculation from Heliocentric Astrology or Geocentric, the influence of Uranus and Saturn, two slow moving planets, will have the same effect.

Bad trade, restricting influences, depression in business, and decline of exports made their effects as marked in Northern Ireland as they have done in England in recent years and will continue to do so for many years to come.

Unemployment will increase, accompanied by strikes and riots in all the manufacturing centres. Taxes will be on the upward grade and stringency of money general.

Trouble with the Customs or increase of Customs duties may be expected between Northern Ireland and the Irish Free State, and considerable friction will result.

The Irish Free State, depending more on its Agricultural products and exports, will be under better conditions, but the same stringency of money that will affect the Northern Counties will also prevent the Southern Counties from making much headway.

Uranus, however, will be favourable for the large electric works recently established

[1] Extract from "The Earth in the Heavens," by L. Edward Johndro.

to harness the river Shannon; also for inventions in connection with some new form of transport, and some novel idea of augmenting revenue by such methods as Lotteries, sweepstakes and such like.

The Political situation will, however, not be favourable. A new mysterious society, modelled on the lines of the previous Sinn Feiners, will commence activities before the close of 1931. They will not be able to fight in the open against the present Government, but will harass it considerably while waiting for the opportunity to declare for complete separation from England.

That opportunity will come in the next European war if Great Britain allows herself to be drawn into it.

Some unusual phenomena are likely to occur in Ireland during the years 1931–32, such as "land-slides," moving bogs, earth tremors, and some extinct volcano will show signs of eruption.[1]

INDIA

When I first wrote this book, "World Predictions," published in 1927, I said on

[1] The Public Press of June 16, 1931, announced that: "the Sliekemakilla Mountain, in County Leitrim, is erupting great volumes of thick black slime, covering the country for several miles round.

"The stuff has a most disagreeable odour and in some sections made road traffic impossible."

page 41: "India will have serious failures of crops, riots among the people, religious disturbances and general upheaval."

Since I wrote those words, I am sorry to say there is no improvement, astrologically, in the outlook for India, as far as England is concerned.

India, in the most ancient works on Astrology, has always been set down as ruled by the Zodiacal Sign of Capricorn—the House of Saturn (positive), and the exaltation of Mars. This becomes of deep portent when one considers that in the Horoscope of King George V, the Sign of Capricorn, at the moment of birth, was posited in the zenith, or highest point, with his ascendant in Aries, the House of Mars, (positive). The planets Mars and Saturn are considered the most menacing and baleful of all, indicating that his reign would be a critical one, associated with wars, revolutions and troubles, especially in connection with countries ruled by the same Zodiacal signs, or by the planets associated with them.

India, under the Sign of Capricorn, with its ruler Saturn, being one of the most prized possessions of the British Throne, must, in consequence, play a most important role during His Majesty's reign. In his Consort's—Queen Mary—Horoscope, the

Zodiacal Sign of Aquarius, called the second House of Saturn, is on the ascendant, foreshadowing that India would be almost equally important in her case.

The Prince of Wales has also the Sign of Aquarius on his Ascendant.

The planets Uranus and Neptune play an important part in influencing the destiny of India, especially in the years from 1929 to about the year of 1935.

There will be no less than five Eclipses of the Sun and Moon during the year of 1931; the majority of them occur in the Signs of Aries and Libra, in union with Uranus. These will be of great importance in connection with England (governed by Aries), and the Far East, generally (governed by Libra).

There is no likelihood of peace in India. On the contrary, sedition and upheavals of all kinds, will be more prevalent than ever. Any attempt at settlement of the Indian question by the British Government will be frustrated and come to nothing.

Women, from now on, will play a large part in the affairs of India. They will throw themselves, heart and soul, into the cause of freedom from British rule.

Although by nature of an extremely gentle and retiring disposition, the women of India, once aroused, will surprise the world by their tenacity of purpose, strength of determination and spirit of martyrdom.

Thousands upon thousands will suffer prison gladly in their effort for Indian independence. They will prevent and block, in every imaginable way, plans made by the British Administration; bringing disorder and chaos in all departments of Government.

British ruling classes, together with the Military and Police Services, will be at their wits' end to circumvent the tide of woman's influences that will steadily and increasingly rise against them. It is a woman's Age that is coming; it is a woman's War that will sweep India from side to side.

The Mahatma Gandhi, with his doctrine of "passive resistance," has let loose a force in India against which bayonets, bullets and bombs will be of no avail.

The boycott of English goods and everything English will increase in strength, year by year. Trade with England will practically cease; goods that necessity may force the Country to buy will be imported from other lands. Japan will seize the opportunity to increase her shipping with Indian ports.

Indians, themselves, will reconstruct a Mercantile Marine, that, in recent years, was forced off the sea by English competition.

The Parsees (the Jews of the East), although to-day a small community, will develop cotton mills and other industries to fill the needs of the vast multitude of people by whom they are surrounded.

On account of their not mingling with politics, they will be assisted by all parties in India and will maintain a certain balance of order in the general upheaval.

The religious laws will become widened to meet the demands of the "new age."

Brahmin priests will find new translations of Buddha's precepts to fit in with the times.

Even the "caste" system will slowly alter to allow India to awaken to the call of the Aquarian influence spreading over the entire world.

The great Princes of India, who have held their Thrones and Independent States by the grace of England, will, one by one, come to the side of their own people and espouse the cause of the freedom of their race.

The "guns of the great War," even in their destructive voices, heralded the approach *of a new era that nothing in the world can resist.*

The Age of Pisces, with its ruler Jupiter —the God of Domination—is coming to a close, the dawn of Aquarius, with its ruler Saturn—symbol of Human Justice—*has already commenced.*

The cycle of Pisces, nearly two thousand years ago, ushered in the dawn of Christianity.

Its period in the Precession of the Equinox is two thousand one hundred and fifty years—*it has nearly run its course.*

Christianity forsook the teachings of "the gentle Christ" for *the domination of the Church.* For the sake of power, it allied itself with Kings and Emperors; with their fall "the Church" of all religions must also fall.

The much prophesied period of the Anti-Christ will, for the time being, come into its own.

Under the reign of Saturn, materialism will, at first, rule supreme. The Great God Moloch will devour his own children. Chaos, destruction, crime and cruelty will race to worship at his brazen feet.

No God but Self will be emblazoned across the skies. And yet, when the reign of Saturn at the commencement of the "new age," has passed away; when humanity is sickened by its trial of "Human Justice"; when it has tried to destroy "the soul of things" and failed; then, and only then, *will the secret symbol of Aquarius be understood*—"the old man";—the man of experience—the man of wisdom—"pouring from his pitcher water upon the earth."

If this, then, is the "voice of the Heavens," how can England hope to hold India; a country that, in the events that are coming, will respond more to the Aquarian influence than, perhaps, any other.

No! England with all her power, might just as well "tell the sea to go back," or the moon to stand still, as to attempt to stem the planetary forces that, for the time being, are arrayed against her.

The population of India, as given by the most recent published census, is, roughly, three hundred and nineteen million, of which about seventy million live in the Independent States ruled over by their own Princes and Maharajahs.

The Mohammedan population is about one hundred and seventy million, constituting a difficult problem from a religious point of view.

That Buddhists and Mohammedans will join together to make India a united nation, is out of the question. The utmost one can hope for is that, in a native government, they would form opposition parties and so rule the country together. The danger is, however, a form of religious-civil war that will keep the country in a state of continual upheaval.

But whatever may happen to the future internal systems of India, the one thing that becomes more and more evident is, that England will not be able to hold that country in subjection as she has done in the past. The best thing she could do would be to give India her Independence and make that vast country with its teeming millions a friend, and not an enemy.

SOUTH AFRICA

The influence of Mars and Saturn in connection with the Cape Colony and the Transvaal will soon make their effects felt.

Unrest of the populace, dissatisfaction with the Government, failure of crops, stringency in the circulation of money and bad trade, will awaken Socialism and its red brother, Communism, in all the principal Cities and Towns of South Africa.

The Dutch, Boer and German element will come more and more to the front. This, although not likely to result in War, will bring about antagonism to British interests and will be adverse to British trade.

Towards the end of 1931 and the early part of 1932, a new national party will be formed in the Transvaal, strongly antagonistic to the Government at Cape Town, and considerable friction will result between these two sections of the country.

South Africa and Africa generally will not advance rapidly like the rest of the world. Some hundreds of years must yet pass before its real wealth will be discovered.

AUSTRALIA AND NEW ZEALAND

Australia is now coming under the influence of the afflicted planets of Uranus, Saturn and Jupiter. A curious situation of contradictory elements will arise.

From now on, for some years, extraordinary weather conditions may be expected, with failure, loss of crops and general stagnation of business. Great droughts may be expected and heavy mortality among her vast herds of cattle.

Exports will fall lower than recent years and the trade in wool will be seriously affected.

Serious fires in several of the large Cities will cause considerable destruction and many banking and business failures are threatened.

The Labour question will become increasingly difficult. Communist activity will spread through the country and serious riots will take place, especially in Melbourne, Brisbane and Sydney.

Against this, some sensational discoveries of natural wealth will be made which will attract widespread attention.

Large numbers of Japanese will endeavour to enter the country. The immigration question will become a delicate problem for the Government, in which Japan, as a Nation, will become involved.

Violent cyclones, with severe earthquakes will occur with unusual frequency during the coming years, and some unusual phenomenon of nature is indicated.

New Zealand will come under similar conditions, with increased danger from earthquakes, storms and tidal waves, especially in relation to the Northern Island.

CENTRAL EUROPE

(*Considered Generally*)

Viewing Europe from an astrological standpoint, I regret to state that similar planetary conditions are appearing exactly as they were a few years before the outbreak of the Great War at the end of July, 1914. The difference being that the prestige of England to prevent War is not so great to-day as it was then.

To-day, Great Britain is more likely to be dragged into the conflict against her will, than enter it from the more heroic standpoint of defending a broken Treaty or fighting for the honour of a "scrap of paper."

Under her altered conditions, Germany will, like England, be more forced into a war than be the aggressor.

For her, it is a question of dying by starvation, or strangulation, or making a bid for freedom on the battlefield. Most decidedly of these two evils, she will choose the latter. Her age long history has been one of recuperation and vitality. From the days of Julius Caesar, conquering hordes have ravaged her territory; sooner or later to be beaten back or forced to come to terms.

Napoleon, with the most famous Army Europe ever brought together, reduced her to serfdom only to meet her again under Blücher at Waterloo.

In the War of 1870, France saw her at the gates of Paris. In 1914 she came within fifteen miles of the French Capital, and if England and her sons from the Colonies had not intervened, there is no doubt France would have been again conquered.

After a war lasting three and a half years, it took fourteen nations to bring Germany to her knees.

It is true she lost her battleships—perhaps a blessing in disguise. It is true she has been humbled to the dust and forced to pay thousands of millions in war indemnity and reparations. It is also true that she has had to rebuild French towns and villages and put them in a better condition than they ever were before; to send enormous quantities of her coal, iron and chemicals to France and to impoverish her own people by doing so.

Yet Germany is not crushed. In the last few years she has built a Zeppelin to go round the world. A commercial Air Service, the largest in Europe; together with scientific discoveries of the greatest benefit to humanity. Her scientists will make such advances in chemical knowledge that they will protect German cities from destruction by attacks from enemy Air Forces.

Prevented from building battleships, she constructed a Mercantile Liner that wrested the "blue ribbon of the Atlantic" from England, the greatest ship-builder in the world. She launched a ten thousand ton cruiser in 1931 equal to any battle-cruiser of twice its size.

She has done all this in ten years, after the most devastating war Europe has ever seen; after losing two million of her sons; after crushing taxations, she has done more than any other nation has ever done before.

Unbroken in spirit, but staggering under her burden, I foresee that Destiny is shaping her into other combinations that will, in the end, make her the most powerful nation in Europe.

In 1926 she made a commercial treaty with Soviet Russia. She could not dare make anything else. She is on the verge of making a similar one with her old allies of Austria-Hungary and, in spite of French opposition, I predict she *will* make it.

Some pact agreement with Italy is also likely during the run of 1931.

A friendly Labour Government in England will favour her plans.

Revolution may, at times, burst like fireworks in her hands, but only to stimulate the blood in her veins; to quicken her for *the greater purpose that lies beyond.*

As Germany's Zodiacal ruler is Mars, in the Sign of Aries, the conjunction of Neptune and Mars being in June, 1931, will be of great importance to the people of Germany. Serious riots are likely to take place, but under them or with them, some military organisation will make its appearance and galvanise the entire nation into a united mass.

This organisation produced by Mars will, for strength and self-protection, tend for an alliance with a country ruled by Saturn —Russia.

A combination of Mars and Saturn will, in the end, produce war, but one favourable to the united interests of Germany and Russia.

Owing to the slow movement of the planet Saturn, the immediate effect of this combination may be delayed, but as this planet becomes stationary in the heavens at the end of September, 1931, and, as many of the Eclipses will occur in Libra (October), some great outbreak in connection with these two countries may be expected.

France and Italy (as countries), being ruled by the Zodiacal Sign of Leo (a Sign in the Zodiac in opposition to the House of Saturn), are likely to become involved in the coming War in Europe, and it is probable they will, about the same time, be in conflict with one another.

The countries in Europe that will be the most disturbed by Planetary conditions during 1931 and immediate following years, will be the following: France, Germany, Italy, Austria, Roumania, Poland, Spain and the Balkan States.

Russia, with her ruler Saturn, passing through its own Zodiacal Sign, will expand in power, wealth and position.

Spain is due to make great changes in her constitutional laws and will commence an era of expansion and general advancement. She will, however, have trouble in her North African possessions and a rebellion of the Riffs is indicated.

Italy will extend her territory in North Africa, to the detriment of France. Dissension and friction between the Vatican and Italian Government will increase.

Mussolini's life will be in danger in the

early months of 1932, and some deep laid plot against him will be discovered.

The South of France and the Riviera will be much disturbed and some phenomenon of nature, such as a severe earthquake, is apparently indicated.

During 1931 and 1932, extensive earthquake shocks will pass through Portugal, Spain, the South of France, Italy, the Balkan States, Macedonia and the South of Russia. In a northerly direction, earthquakes will effect Northern France, England, Norway and Sweden.

Turkey will make rapid strides towards advancement, both politically and in social reforms, but some extraordinary religious changes may be expected.

Palestine and Syria will come under disturbing influences and considerable bloodshed there and in Irak will result. Zionism will increase in power and the Jewish settlement question will excite attention in both the United States and in England.

Egypt will unite in opposition to English control; a sensational attempt to interfere with the Suez Canal will be attempted and Great Britain will be forced to pour troops into that country to protect her interests.

THE U.S.A. AND THE WESTERN HEMISPHERE

The United States began an adverse planetary period about the Fall of 1929 which is likely to last until the Spring of 1932. There is not much likelihood of any great improvement in the internal affairs of the country before then.

The influence of Saturn in adverse aspect to Uranus, is the cause of the restrictions of trade, decline of exports and the extraordinary wave of depression that affected and will affect nearly all classes during this period.

The planet Uranus has great importance at the present period in connection with the United States. Its influence is particularly noticeable in connection with the Stock Markets in New York, and its inter-connection with the Exchanges in the other large cities, producing bad conditions all over the country. Owing to the position of Uranus in opposition to Saturn, it breeds fear and nervousness in the minds of people, causing panics, runs on banks, chaos and confusion.

Extraordinary fluctuations in the price of Stocks and Shares are likely to prevail in the United States for some time. Dividends will shrink or be passed by even some of the largest business concerns, and a general stringency of money will be one of the main features of the present period.

Unemployment will have to be seriously taken in hand by the Government at Washington and ways and means devised to cope with the situation.

The position of Neptune favours Communist propaganda, sedition, riots and destruction of property, together with a "crime-wave" that will sweep the country from side to side.

The Government will be severely censured by the Press and public for its procrastination in dealing with important matters concerning home affairs, and a general feeling of unrest and dissatisfaction will make itself manifest in every State of the Union.

In one way, the position of Uranus is favourable to the United States, in the stimulation of inventions, especially those relating to electricity, wireless and radio improvements, aeroplanes, airships and such like.

About the end of 1931 and the early months of 1932, some practical plan for a fuller utilisation of power extracted from coal will be made in the Western States, which is likely to revolutionise the treatment of coal in all countries.

Great engineering plans will be carried into effect in the United States in the next few years, such as the opening up of waterways, the harnessing of rivers for irrigation purposes and electrical development on a large scale.

Some sweeping changes will soon be made in connection with the Divorce Laws and the Prohibition question.[1]

The Presidential Election in 1932 will be marked by intense bitterness between the Democratic and Republican parties. Opposition will augment against President Hoover and the chances against his being re-elected are likely to increase.

During the latter part of 1931 and the early months of 1932, Americans living in China will be in a position of considerable danger. American battleships will be sent into Chinese waters and a danger of war will result.

MEXICO, CENTRAL AMERICA AND THE LATIN STATES OF SOUTH AMERICA

(*Considered Generally*)

Mexico has for its Zodiacal Ruler, the Sign of Capricorn (House of Saturn,—*positive*). In many ways it will be like Russia and India in its unsettled conditions, upheavals,

[1] American newspapers in May 1931 stated that Two Billion 848 million dollars was paid yearly by the people of the United States for intoxicating liquor and "Boot legging" as an Industry is now equal to the manufacture of Automobiles.

periodical revolutions; and, like the above named countries, it will rebel against religious thraldom, all forms of ecclesiastical domination and interference from outside countries.[1]

Russia, however, having for its Zodiacal Ruler, the Sign of Aquarius (House of Saturn,—negative), and Uranus, will recover more quickly from revolutions or disaster and will advance more rapidly towards the achievement of its purpose than will Mexico or India.

THE CENTRAL STATES; GUATEMALA, HONDURAS, SALVADOR, NICARAGUA, COSTA RICA AND PANAMA, will be greatly afflicted by earthquakes during the next seven years.

Great changes in Government and many revolutions are indicated for the Latin-American States of South America during 1931 and the following ten years. Their exports will shrink in volume, and great distress and unemployment will prevail.

On the Pacific Ocean side of South America, an earthquake zone will increase in intensity, passing through Chile, Peru, the Panama and Central America, expending its forces

[1] On June 7, 1931, the American Press published the information that "the Government of Mexico had made plans to create a military reserve of one million trained men with a scheme that involves Military training in all public schools, even in Kindergartens where children will be taught with toy soldiers and given other preparatory training."

in the direction of New York and the Eastern States of the U.S.A.

On the opposite side of the Pacific, many destructive earthquakes are likely to occur in Japan, with recurrent tidal waves causing damage along the Californian Coast.

Submerged and unknown islands will, during 1931, and following years, rise on the East and Western Coasts of South America. Earlier in this book I have stated that earthquake upheavals in coming years will cause the lost continent of Atlantis to be discovered.

In recent years a new volcano suddenly appeared off the coast of Ecuador and is now recorded in the U.S. Navy Department at San Francisco.

On June 14, 1931 the Press announced that: "two new islands have been discovered off the Brazilian coast by the Commander of the English steamer Lelande."

PART III

COMING EARTHQUAKES, SUBSIDENCES AND UPHEAVALS

FOR many years I have made a study of earthquakes in various parts of the world. I have traced backwards through history to find if there could be some possible clue to what might be called earthquake cycles or epochs of time when great upheavals took place in the past and when such alterations in the earthcrust would be likely to occur again.

It would be too difficult in a book of this nature to explain the various theories I have examined, or go deeply into the records of the various parts of the earth that have been more afflicted by upheavals than others.

So many civilisations have been swept away by the obliterating march of time that there is no reliable world history to build upon. It is only by a study of the shattered monuments of the past with traces they have left of long dead civilisations that one is able to grasp some idea—even though it may be a faint one—of the great cataclysms of Nature that have taken place in the world from time to time.

History may lead us back over a mere space of a few thousand years—and speak of nations that rose and fell before the infancy of our own, but beyond Greece and Rome, history is already lost in legend and mythical romance, and the seeker becomes appalled at the night of antiquity that lies beyond.

Egypt, Persia, India, China, tell of ages so far beyond our dreams that we wake with wonder and beg to get more light, but they themselves have lost their history, and point to silent monuments whose only language is a piece of broken stone.

Beyond the days of the great Pharaoh legend speaks of a lost Atlantis and whispers of a cataclysm that cost a continent and brought an ocean into being.

Man discovered a new hemisphere. He called it "the new world" until in clearing its undergrowth he stumbled on ruins that not even legend seemed to know existed.[1]

Science tells of "a glacial age" and teaches that Europe was at one time buried in ice—at the same time she discovers remains of tropical plants at the North Pole and science joins us in asking—why?

Humanity in all ages set up a question mark and called it—God.

[1] Recent discoveries in Central America tell of cities which flourished before even the Maya period.

As we cannot get help from history—let us see if Nature will come to our aid. Very humbly we knock at her portals. Timidly we cross her threshold—we know Nature is very old, that she existed at the "beginning of things"—she alone may be able to explain.

At first we cannot find her—she is surrounded by so many millions of workers that we are afraid of becoming lost. We enter workshop after workshop, all are too busy to notice our questioning glance, and so we pass from one to the other. It is the same story wherever we go. Never ending work, never ending creation, never ending destruction—birth and death in the same moment, past, present and eternity moulding in their hands our wonderful world.

Going still farther into the "workshop of things," furnaces create jewels, gold creeps through rocks, oils and rare minerals gather into pockets, crystals take on shape, and molecules strive for perfection.

In our amazement we again ask to see Nature—we want to meet her face to face.

First the smallest atom answers "I am Nature," then the worm at our feet, then the jewel in the mass of rock, then the rock itself, a volcano trembles with its effort for speech, an earthquake crashes for a thousand miles, storm, sea, earth, heaven, all answer "I am Nature and Nature is—God."

Taking this explanation for our foundation, let us now regard the question of upheavals and earthquakes as purely natural occurrences, and endeavour to find out why they are likely to appear in certain periods and not in others.

In the first place we must make an effort to lay aside prejudice and get the fact established in our minds, that this earth of ours, although comparatively small in relation to other planets, *is differently constituted to all the others*, and in its particular scope is next the Sun in importance in the solar system of which our earth forms part.

It is no use our decrying our world by saying it is insignificant in comparison to other worlds and systems whirling through space. There is nothing without purpose in the marvellous mechanism of the heavens, and whether we care to regard the question from a religious standpoint or not, it is admitted by all persons who have a logical mind that there must be a "First Cause" behind creation—and if there is a "First Cause" why not also *—a purpose.*

Without going into the question at length or bringing the many arguments to bear on the subject that might be brought, I must here state that all the scientific knowledge at our disposal teaches, that the influence of the Sun, the planets and that mysterious pathway through the heavens called the Zodiac, control life on this earth of ours, and *were purposely created to do so.*

Changes of climate and all conditions relating to our planet are the direct outcome of the celestial influences brought to bear on it—the most important of all being the effect of "the Precession of the Equinoxes" to which I have alluded in previous chapters. It is the effect of "the precess" in its relation to the earthquake zone of belts of the earth that I am only going to write about here.

It has been scientifically established by modern astronomers as well as ancient students of the heavens that the "Precession of the Equinoxes" causes an alteration in the polar axis of the earth, and that in consequence the Sun retrogrades through every sign of the Zodiac, and in a period of time calculated as 2150 years passes out of one sign and enters another.

It is this alteration of the axis of the earth that, in my judgment, brings about great cyclic changes affecting the balance of the earth and so causes earthquake zones to alter their direction. By the gigantic changes and upheavals thus created they bring about such alterations in climate that "tropical" parts become "temperate" and "temperate" change to "tropical" in the course of time.

Entire races have been known to suddenly

abandon a country where they had for thousands of years previously developed their civilisations. In different parts of India, Siam and China, huge migrations have taken place leaving cities and palaces deserted behind them. In Cambodia ruins of ancient civilisations have recently been discovered having no relation whatever to the present inhabitants of that country.

In India some of these deserted cities are enormous, together with wonderful palaces that are to-day nothing more than magnificent ruins. In Central America the Maya race have as completely disappeared as if they never existed—the only record left being gigantic ruins of stone, which could only have been broken into the condition they are in by some colossal earthquake or cataclysm that we can only imagine.

Important traces of early life on the Northern Continent of America have, in recent years, attracted considerable attention. The British United Press sent the following interesting account from Washington which appeared lately in the *Sunday Times* of London:

"Evidence which, it is declared, shows that the most ancient man yet discovered in the world lived in what is now the United States 4,000,000 years ago, is claimed to have been found by Dr. Harold J. Cook, the palæontologist of Denver (Colorado).

"In view of the belief held by scientists for years that America was devoid of the remains of prehistoric man, Dr. Cook's discoveries are of great importance.

"Long before the ice age enveloped the northern hemisphere in a mantle of snow and ice, the northern United States, Canada, and Alaska were a Paradise, it was shown by fossils uncovered by Dr. Cook and his associates from the Colorado Museum of Natural History in Denver.

"Dr. Cook's discovery of evidence and remains of man in the United States was made at Agate Springs, Nebraska. Deep in a quarry quantities of fossilised prehistoric animal bones were found. Among them, Dr. Cook came upon bone implements which, he says, were fashioned by human hands.

"The most important discovery, however, was even more human than that of the ape man discovered in Java.

"Because of its association with the prehistoric bones and with the fossilised tools, scientists believe that the tooth belonged at one time to a man living ages ago, so far back that in comparison to him the American Indians were the veriest of newcomers."

That great multitudes of people at times abandon *en masse* large tracts of country that suffer from earthquakes, is shown even in our own days. In the accounts recently published of the effects of seismic shocks in parts of Japan, it is stated that in many cases towns severely damaged will never be rebuilt on account of their inhabitants leaving those districts.

A similar effect has been reported as the result of the recent earthquakes in Southern Russia, and the Crimea, where wholesale migration has also occurred.

To realise what the complete abandoning of a town or place means, one need only journey as far as San Remo in Italy. An easy carriage drive takes the visitor to one of the loveliest bits of scenery perhaps in the world. In the distance one sees a town with long winding streets, the usual Market Square with its church of the Madonna, the bell that called to prayer still hangs in the belfry—above it, the Crucifix of the Saviour.

In those streets now covered with grass not a footstep is heard, doors swing open on their hinges, bits of curtains still sway in the windows—but silence everywhere, not even the song of a bird seems to be heard.

In February, 1887, this little town of Bussana was full of life. Men thronged the market place with their baskets of olives and fruit, women sat in their doorways chattering and happy children played round their feet.

A Sunday evening came, the bell tolled the hour of Vespers, candles were lit on the altar, the priest and the congregation joined in the prayers. Without warning, the sudden roar of an earthquake was heard, the place rocked as if made of cards, the roof of the church fell with a crash—hundreds lay beneath its timbers—outside the houses crumbled, yawning chasms opened, swallowing men, women and children. The moans of the injured and dying rent the air, and the blackness of night and death hung like a pall over the scene.

When morning came those that were left crept like hunted animals from the place—not one of them ever returned to live there again; they built another town some miles away. The grass grown streets will never be trodden again, except by a few travellers who, like myself, are drawn to such a spot to wonder at the mysteries of Nature.

This is a slight illustration of how seismic disasters may be the cause of migrations of people that produce far reaching effects.

Following out the theory that the "Precession of the Equinoxes" alters the axis of the poles, and so produces world changes, in a preceding chapter I have given calculations to show that we are at the present time a little over a hundred and sixty years in the new zodiacal sign of Aquarius. Consequently, during a little over a century and a half, important world changes have been taking place and must be expected to take place.

The more pronounced "lean-over" or tilt of the axis of the earth, it is logical to assume, produces new zones of earthquake activity and the reopening of long closed fissures which affect countries where earthquakes have been considered "things of the past."

This theory is amply demonstrated by recent earth tremors in such places as Northern

France, the Channel Islands, and Great Britain, also by so-called extinct volcanoes becoming again active, together with the rise in the bed of oceans.

As a proof of the remarkable changes which have taken place recently, I will draw attention to the following:

A return of volcanic activity to Mount McKinley, one of the highest mountains in the United States (20,300 feet). The eruption of Mount Sheshadin in the Aleutian Islands on the 11th November, 1925. Since this volcanic activity great changes have been noticed in Alaska which from having an extreme polar climate has become warmer than many parts of the Eastern States—an experience not before known in records concerning this country. Where was usually ice and snow has, in recent years, become covered with vegetation, together with a remarkable decrease of glaciers never known before.

Reports from the University of Norway show that great changes have taken place in the climate of the Arctic Ocean since 1860. Great masses of ice and glaciers that were considered unchangeable have completely disappeared, and even fish belonging to waters far more South have recently been found in Arctic waters.

A new volcano, according to the San Francisco *Chronicle* of January 18th, 1926, has been discovered off the coast of Ecuador, and is now recorded in the U.S. Navy Department of San Francisco.

Mauna Loa in the Hawaiian Islands, a volcano which has given no signs of activity in recent years, suddenly burst into violent eruption on the evening of the 17th April, 1926.

Since the great earthquake of San Francisco in 1908, there has been continued seismic activity along the western coast of America through Japan and China on the other side of the Pacific, and numerous submarine disturbances—while on the eastern side of America important changes have been taking place, and the floor of the Atlantic Ocean has risen alarmingly in many places. The Bay of Biscay which was at one time two miles and a half in depth, is to-day in some places less than 150 feet deep.

In a report made in 1924 by the Eastern Cable Company on the break of one of their cables between the island of St. Helena and the Cape, it was found that the broken cable which was laid in 1899 in water over three miles deep was found in 1924 to be lying on the ocean bed at a depth *of only three-quarters of a mile*, showing the rapid rise in the floor of the sea in a period of twenty-five years.

These submarine upheavals in their turn affect the great ocean currents and consequently the Gulf Stream, which is of the most vital importance to such countries as Iceland, Ireland, Great Britain, Norway, Sweden, Germany, France, and Spain. Without the warming flow of the Gulf Stream such countries would quickly become covered with ice, and all vegetation would cease.

Geologists and scientists are now in agreement that the Glacial period which covered Europe as far down as the Mediterranean took place between 15,000 to 18,000 years ago. During the same period ice covered the whole of Canada and the United States as far south as Illinois, which lies at about the same parallel as the Mediterranean in Europe. Even still more important, and what has greater bearing on my argument that from time to time the axis of the earth is so completely tilted that civilisation is swept off certain portions of the earth, are the proofs advanced by scientists that the Glacial Age of 15,000 years ago was only one of many similar Ice Ages that the earth has passed through in its long history, and further, that between these great Glacial periods the climate in those countries appears to have swung back again to semi-tropical conditions, so much so that "in Scandinavia the mammoth roamed in forests of birch, pine and spruce, together with the *Elephas Antiquus* resembling the Indian elephant."[1]

[1] "Evolution of Climate," by C. E. P. Brooks, M.Sc., etc.

If such a swing of the pendulum took place at different periods before, is it not reasonable to expect that it will occur again, and again, and yet again, in the history of a world that science proves has existed for millions of years and may exist equally for as many millions of ages to come?

If one were to tell the average Britisher that England, together with Wales and Scotland, has been severely shaken by earthquakes in the past, and is just as likely to be as equally shaken in the future, he would lift his eyebrows with incredulity and disbelief. In spite of this, however, authentic records show that from the year A.D. 1048 to January, 1924, one thousand, one hundred and ninety earthquakes took place.[1] These records do not include after-shocks or tremors.

Of all countries in the world, Ireland is the most free from earthquakes. For every 1,000 British earthquakes only 43 originated in Ireland.

The weakest part of the earth's strata is undoubtedly a zone or belt lying 40 degrees of latitude both above and below the Equator.

The Northern part of the belt passes through Japan, the middle States of North America, through Spain, Italy, Turkey, Asia Minor, Persia, India and China. It affects all

[1] This number is exclusive of earthquake shocks in Ireland and the Channel.

countries from 40 degrees down to the Equator. The Southern part passes through the Argentine, South Africa, South Australia and New Zealand, and affects all countries from the 40 latitude up to the Equator.

This zone has two great centres of activity, one East in or about Japan, and the other situated in the West in or about Mexico, Central America and the Isthmus of Panama.

Any disturbance in one of these centres is carried by this belt from one side of the globe to the other. This central zone radiates earthquakes, shocks and tremors through fissures or cracks in the earth's crust, extending for thousands of miles in every direction.

These fissures have a zig-zag formation, like forked lightning, and follow the course of least resistance through the rocky outer crust of the earth. Under some circumstances they exhaust or spend their force through vent holes such as volcanoes, which accounts in a large majority of cases for the activity of volcanoes both before or after a seismic disturbance.

The recent crop of earthquakes in Japan was followed by a marked increase of volcanic activity in Mexico, followed by shocks in Czecho-Slovakia and Southern Russia.

Forty-eight hours after the submarine disturbance off the coast of Japan, where a tidal wave caused enormous damage to the Island of Formosa in August, 1927, one of the worst shocks known in recent years took place in the neighbourhood of Odessa and the Crimea, and newspapers described an extraordinary phenomenon in the Black Sea, "where a sheet of flame appeared to burst through the water and the bottom of the sea sank over 700 feet."[1]

That this earthquake belt or zone I have alluded to has become more marked during the past 100 to 150 years, is the considered opinion of scientists, and many theories have been put forward to account for earth tremors and quakes that have recently taken place in countries more or less immune from such things, such as the British Isles.

In *The Morning Post* of London under the date of the 16th September, 1927, the following leading article appeared under the menacing heading of "A Crack in the Crust":

"It was inevitable that the frequent occurrence of earthquakes during the last twelve months should suggest some theory to account for the sequence; and now the hypothesis is put forward, on high authority, that what has been happening in recent years is a crack in the crust of the earth, due to surface shrinkage by cooling. It would seem that the earthquakes of recent years have followed a well-defined line, north of, but roughly parallel to the Equator, passing from San Francisco across the Pacific to Japan, and thence through Turkestan, the Black Sea, and Messina, across Southern Europe and the North Atlantic. The typhoons and tidal waves which the world has been experiencing are to b

[1] "Daily Express" and other papers, Sept. 16th and 17th, 192

regarded as secondary effects of the seismic disturbances, and some observers have been bold enough to predict that before the end of the year there will occur a very severe earthquake on the line of cracking already so well marked."

That there is an unusual number of seismic disturbances in these recent years is reflected in the many references to them now appearing in the Press. The London *Star* called 1923 "The year of Trembling," and printed the following interesting account under the heading of "Earth's Great Convulsions during 1923":

"What is wrong with the crust of the earth?

"It has never been more disturbed by seismic tremors in the recollection of this generation, and the year 1923 will long be remembered as the earthquake year.

"When to this is added typhoons, waterspouts, tidal waves, big fires, and other disasters, it is not surprising that the superstitious and the credulous are turning to some connection with the world-war.

"The expounders of prophecy are beginning to cite again those passages in the Apocalyptic Scriptures which couple earthquakes with war, pestilence, and famine as the signs of the last days of the present dispensation.

"The cause of the great earthquakes lies in the gradually solidifying lower strata of this vast ball. In some of them huge masses of rock 40 miles long and 20 broad have slipped a cog and moved for some distance, carrying with them all the strata above them. This means that the whole face of landscapes is changed.

"Quite apart from the destruction of buildings which accompany earthquakes like those of Lisbon, San Francisco, and Tokio, there are great fissures in the earth. In the Assam (India) earthquake of 1897 some of these cracks in the soil could be traced for 12 miles across country. The course of rivers was changed, lakes 20 ft. deep appeared where there had been dry land, and hills sunk so that a clear view was obtainable which previously had been interrupted.

"The extent to which the subterranean landslides spread is shown by the Japanese scientists' report that the centre of the recent disaster was a point under the sea 62 miles south of Tokio.

"The notable feature of the year's earthquakes is that, as usual, a very large proportion of them happened in countries which are close to the sea coast. That is in accordance with history—Lisbon, Concepcion (Chili), Valparaiso, Tokio, Messina, to name but a few that occur to memory among the great earthquakes of the last two centuries, are all islands or on the sea coast.

"The same thing happened in regard to the list of this year's quakes. We have Naples, Ancona, and other Italian ports, the Azore Islands, several in Hawaii, another island, Kamschatka, and islands in the China Sea.

"Malta has been twice visited, and the islands of Majorca in the Mediterranean and St. Helena in the Atlantic are also in the list of the affected areas. Los Angeles, on the Californian coast, is in the list, and so is Thessaly.

"On the other side, earthquakes far from the sea, we have only Assam, Tibet, Turkestan, Persia and Asia Minor.

"COMATOSE VOLCANOES

"There is no doubt that this list gives a great deal of *prima facie* support to the idea that the primary cause of earthquakes is the entrance of sea-water into the craters of supposedly extinct or comatose volcanoes. If owing to leakage large quantities of sea-water penetrate suddenly into the deeper strata which are still in a state of great heat, it is not surprising that the convulsions of the overlying strata many hundred of feet in depth should be vast in area and colossal in effects.

"Obviously this will not account for earthquakes like that of Assam, but it is a theory to which a great deal of attention has always been directed by scientists. The persistent historical connection between earthquakes and volcanoes and islands is one that it is impossible to overlook."

What is called "subsidence" in England has in recent years caused considerable alarm, as is shown in the following article which appeared in the *Daily Express* of the 11th September, 1927:

"MYSTERY CRACKS IN BRITAIN'S CRUST.

"ALARM CAUSED BY LANDSLIDES AND COLLAPSES.

"What is happening to the surface of Britain? This question is being raised everywhere following a period in which scarcely a day passes without a landslide, a subsidence, or a building collapse being reported.

"Alarm has been caused by crumbling roads, sliding hills, and sinking railway lines in many parts of the country, while houses and business premises in London and the provinces have come crashing down, often without warning.

"Two of the most serious of such disasters were the fall of a house in Beak Street, W., in which two people were killed, and the collapse of part of the Commercial Union Assurance Company's seven-storey building in Cornhill on August 6th. In this case a subsidence also occurred under the roadway, necessitating the closing of the thoroughfare."

Calling such things "subsidences" and ignoring the many earthquake shocks which have passed through England during recent years, is, to my mind, similar to the people of San Francisco when anyone makes an allusion to the great earthquake of 1906, immediately saying in a universal chorus "Of course, you mean 'the fire'."

Conclusion

In writing this book it has been my earnest endeavour to keep free from all prejudice as regards nations, countries or religions.

My effort has been to make known the truth of the tendencies of the world as has been given to me, either by Astrological knowledge, by calculations of periodicity, or any occult means at my disposal.

Underlying the pages of this book will be seen my own deeply engrained belief in Divine Design, made manifest in all things.

The Soul of Design is, in itself, *perfection.* Therefore, even its most unconscious effort must be in the end to reproduce *itself in all things.* In obedience to this law, Man—the highest effort of Design on this sphere, is, by the upward urge of ages, *slowly ascending towards perfection.*

Calamities may happen; wars, plagues and pestilence may destroy; nations may rise and fall or new nations be born; but behind all, the mystery of Design weaves, on the tapestry of Time, the pattern of *Purpose.*

As "a thousand years are but a day," in the sight of the Creator, so the greatest span of the greatest nation is but a footstep in the aeons of ages that have preceded it and will come after.

Men, in far gone centuries, built cities of stone they thought, in their pride, would endure forever; they did not reckon that the movement of the Precession of the Equinox would turn seas into lands and sweep their monuments into oblivion.

Mayas, Incas, Egyptians, Persians, Grecians, Romans, all built their Towers of Babel and have passed away.

What if our present "Great" Nations should also pass? What if a change of a few degrees of climate would make Europe uninhabitable, and Paris, Berlin, Moscow and London return to the wastes they were a few thousand years ago?

"Impossible!" some will cry; "God would not allow such a disaster."

In the blindness of their egotism they forget the lessons of Babylon, Nineveh, Memphis, Athens, Ancient Rome, and former "great" nations too numerous to mention.

They forget, also, that they do *not* worship God; that their God is a fetish *they* have created, an imaginary something, fit only to lead their sons into battle, to bless their banners, to pray to for victory, to praise when "the enemy"—their fellow-man—has been annihilated and destroyed.

They forget that the God of Nature is the same God for one race as for another. They forget that He is "no respector of persons," that "He does not dwell in temples made by hands."

They forget that He, Himself, has said: "God is not mocked." And yet, as nations, they mock "Him" all the time.

And so they go on. They create Armies to kill one another, invent "gas" lest some might escape, educate their children to hate other children, poison water that animals may die, pay for and impoverish generations to employ every devilish means of extermination of their brother-man that can be invented.

In the end they wonder that their God "does not hear."

To my way of thinking the greatest mystery of life is—God is *so patient* that the slow tortoise of evolution moves ever on.

Races may die, Empires may fall, Cities may crumble, yet something is gained.

The upward path may be tedious, the track winding and devious, false guides may lose their way, religions may beckon and vanish, but the upward urge remains.

In the light of to-day, we excavate Ur of the Chaldees to find proofs that Abraham, the Father of the Hebrews, *did* exist and that Bible records are true.

We open up Mayan ruins and find a race who worshipped the Sun, the "Lord of Hosts," under another name.

We follow the footsteps of the Incas and learn of a civilisation thousands of years before our own. We turn back to China and marvel at the wisdom that Confucius taught.

We unwind the wrappings of Egyptian mummies to find their belief in an "after-life" and their hope of a resurrection to come.

In all we find the "upward urge" for something higher; the hungry craving of humanity for "betterment"; the age-long climb to know and *to understand*.

For a moment we wonder that the Creative Essence of things, so perfect in itself, did not make all perfect at the commencement. It is Nature, herself, who answers our question: Has not the bud to burst from seed, force itself through clay, resist storm and frost and rain before it can become a flower? And a weed: Has it not the same struggle, even more so? Still stranger,—is it not, that *some weeds* become *flowers through cultivation*. And that "human weeds" obey that same law.

The way of evolution is a long, long road. The school of life has many, many classes. The making of a soul, aeons and aeons of civilisations.

FINIS